DISABILITY AND THE DISABLED - ISSUES, LAWS AND PROGRAMS

STUDENTS WITH DISABILITIES IN THE JUSTICE SYSTEM

EDUCATIONAL NEEDS AND ISSUES

DISABILITY AND THE DISABLED - ISSUES, LAWS AND PROGRAMS

Additional books in this series can be found on Nova's website under the Series tab.

Additional e-books in this series can be found on Nova's website under the e-book tab.

DISABILITY AND THE DISABLED - ISSUES, LAWS AND PROGRAMS

STUDENTS WITH DISABILITIES IN THE JUSTICE SYSTEM

EDUCATIONAL NEEDS AND ISSUES

AMELIA GUERRERO
EDITOR

nova publishers
New York

Additional color graphics may be available in the e-book version of this book.

Library of Congress Cataloging-in-Publication Data

ISBN: 978-1-63483-749-1

Published by Nova Science Publishers, Inc. † New York

CONTENTS

PREFACE

Studies show that up to 85 percent of youth in juvenile detention facilities have disabilities that make them eligible for special education services, yet only 37 percent receive these services while in school. A disproportionate percentage of these detained youth are youth of color. These statistics should lead to the conclusion that many disabled youth in the juvenile justice and criminal justice systems are deprived of an appropriate education that could have changed their School-to-Prison Pipeline trajectory. The "School-to-Prison Pipeline" refers to policies and practices that push our nation's schoolchildren, especially those most at risk, out of classrooms and into the juvenile and criminal justice systems. This pipeline reflects the prioritization of incarceration over education. Yet the benefits of special education are in question. Students with disabilities who receive special education services in school have poorer outcomes and are suspended and expelled more often than their peers without disabilities. This book provides recommendations that address both conscious and unconscious racial biases that combine with disability discrimination to contribute to the crisis

In: Students with Disabilities in the Justice System ISBN: 978-1-63483-749-1
Editor: Amelia Guerrero

Chapter 1

BREAKING THE SCHOOL-TO-PRISON PIPELINE FOR STUDENTS WITH DISABILITIES*

National Council on Disability

ACKNOWLEDGMENTS

The National Council on Disability would like to acknowledge the assistance of the Disability Rights Education and Defense Fund (DREDF) in developing this report and the HSC Foundation in convening our Fall 2014 meeting which contributed significantly to its findings.

SECTION 1: EXECUTIVE SUMMARY

Studies show that up to 85 percent of youth in juvenile detention facilities have disabilities that make them eligible for special education services, yet only 37 percent receive these services while in school.[1] A disproportionate percentage of these detained youth are youth of color. These statistics should

* This is an edited, reformatted and augmented version of a report issued June 18, 2015.
[1] National Council on Disability. "National Disability Policy: A Progress Report." 2011, http://www.ncd.gov/progress_reports/Oct312011#_edn92.

lead to the conclusion that many disabled youth in the juvenile justice and criminal justice systems are deprived of an appropriate education that could have changed their School-to-Prison Pipeline trajectory. The "School-to-Prison Pipeline" refers to policies and practices that push our nation's schoolchildren, especially those most at risk, out of classrooms and into the juvenile and criminal justice systems.[2] This pipeline reflects the prioritization of incarceration over education. Yet the benefits of special education are in question. Students with disabilities who receive special education services in school have poorer outcomes and are suspended and expelled more often than their peers without disabilities.[3] These dire statistics are even worse for students of color with disabilities, who are disproportionately classified as having an emotional disturbance or an intellectual disability and disproportionately segregated.[4]

These realities are often contradictory and confounding:

1) Many students with disabilities, including students of color, go through general education with unidentified and unaddressed academic, behavioral, or mental health needs;
2) Students of color are overrepresented in special education and experience more segregation and worse outcomes; and
3) Students who qualify for special education too often receive inferior services in segregated settings and incur repeated suspensions and expulsions.

---

[2] The American Civil Liberties Union (ACLU). "What is the School-To-Prison Pipeline?" accessed May 1, 2015, https://www.aclu.org/what-school-prison-pipeline.

[3] In 2010–2011, the national graduation rate for students with disabilities was 61 percent, compared to 80 percent for all students. Stetser, Marie C., and Robert Stillwell. "Public High School Four-Year On-Time Graduation Rates and Event Dropout Rates: School Years 2010–11 and 2011–12." April 2014, accessed April 30, 2015, http://nces.ed.gov/pubs2014/2014391.pdf. Moreover, in 2011–2012, students with disabilities were more than twice as likely to receive an out-of-school suspension (13%) than students without disabilities (6%). U.S. Department of Education Office for Civil Rights, "Civil Rights Data Collection, Data Snapshot: School Discipline" Issue Brief, March 2014, accessed April 30, 2015, http://www2.ed.gov/about/offices/list/ocr/docs/crdc-discipline-snapshot.pdf.

[4] Nationally, 36 percent of all African American male secondary students with disabilities were suspended at least once in 2009–2010 compared to 17 percent of white male secondary students with disabilities. Losen, Daniel J., and Tia Elena Martinez. "Out of School and Off Track: The Overuse of Suspensions in American Middle and High Schools." *Civil Rights Project/Proyecto Derechos Civiles* (2013), accessed April 30, 2015, http://civilrightsproject.ucla.edu/resources/projects/center-for-civil-rights-remedies/school-to-prison-folder/federal-reports/out-of-school-and-off-track-the-overuse-of-suspensions-in-american-middle-and-high-schools/OutofSchool-OffTrack_UCLA_4-8.pdf.

In conjunction with its fall quarterly meeting, the National Council on Disability (NCD) convened a stakeholder forum in Atlanta on October 6, 2014, to receive testimony on the role of special education in the School-to-Prison Pipeline and to confront these issues.[5] The meeting began with the following facts, principles, and questions:

FACTS:

- All races have members with disabilities.
- Among incarcerated youth, 85 percent have learning and/or emotional disabilities, yet only 37 percent receive special education in school. Most were either undiagnosed or not properly served in school.
- Many students have invisible disabilities, such as specific learning disability (SLD), emotional disturbance, posttraumatic stress disorder, or attention deficit/hyperactivity disorder (ADHD).
- Schools suspended students with disabilities and students of color at many times the rate of their white counterparts.
- Schools suspend students of color with individualized education plans (IEPs), whether they have disabilities or not, to the most disproportionate degree.

PRINCIPLES:

- We cannot address the School-to-Prison Pipeline without a disability lens.
- Special education is not a place. We are talking about a system of services and supports for inclusion in general education.
- Special educators have developed tools for teaching students with a variety of disabilities, including learning, behavioral, and emotional disabilities.
- A referral for special education assessments can help identify learning, behavior, and emotional needs.
- Students with disabilities and their families need information, training, and leadership development to effectively use the Individuals with Disabilities Education Act (IDEA) as a tool to secure better educational services.

[5] National Council on Disability, 79 Fed. Reg. 56,830 (Sept. 23, 2014).

- There is a need for advocates to assist students with disabilities and their families in securing services and providing oversight to the delivery of services.
- An investment in IDEA, Section 504 of the Rehabilitation Act, and the Americans with Disabilities Act (ADA) is necessary to ensure that youth of color reap the benefits of disability laws.
- Students of color should have access to the benefits of IDEA/504/ADA services to the same extent as white students.

QUESTIONS:

- Does IDEA offer important tools to infuse better educational services for students of color with disabilities who are currently suspended or expelled?
- Can the proper implementation of IDEA help disrupt the School-to-Prison Pipeline for these students?

NCD has concluded that IDEA can and should be an important part of the solution to the School-to-Prison Pipeline crisis. Thus, the recommendations in this report focus on ways to improve existing special education delivery and enforcement systems to better meet the needs of students with disabilities who risk entering the Pipeline.

First and foremost, NCD would like to see a unified system of education with all students educated in the regular education classrooms with special education supports. But improved implementation of disability laws in this manner alone will not eradicate the persistent racial and ethnic disparities within the class of students with disabilities caught in the Pipeline. Thus, the recommendations acknowledge that efforts to break the School-to-Prison Pipeline for students with disabilities must address both conscious and unconscious racial biases that combine with disability discrimination to contribute to the crisis.[6]

[6] Kim, Catherine, Daniel Losen, and Damon Hewitt. 2010. *The School-to-Prison Pipeline: Structuring Legal Reform.* New York: New York University Press.

Summary of Key Findings and Recommendations

Key Findings

- The confusing disciplinary provisions added and refined in the last two IDEA reauthorizations have allowed schools to ignore their overarching obligation to provide a Free and Appropriate Public Education (FAPE), particularly the requirement to consider behavioral supports in the IEP.
- Persistent racial and ethnic disparities in identification, discipline, placement, and other key categories show IDEA implementation breakdowns disproportionately affect students of color with disabilities.
- Although the overall inclusion of students with disabilities in the general education classroom has increased over the last decade, statistics shows that students of color with disabilities remain disproportionately segregated from their peers without disabilities.
- Reports of both overrepresentation and underrepresentation of students of color in special education suggest that child find enforcement does not ensure schools refer and assess these students in a nondiscriminatory manner.
- Racial and ethnic disparities in suspensions and expulsions suggest the presence of unconscious or implicit biases that combine with discrimination on the basis of disability to contribute to the School-to-Prison Pipeline crisis.
- School-wide positive behavior interventions and supports (SWPBIS) and response to intervention (RTI) do not reduce racial and ethnic disparities in discipline without specific attention to issues of race and culture.
- State and local government entities often fail to enforce and comply with mandatory data collection and reporting laws.

Key Recommendations

- The U.S. Departments of Education (ED) and Justice (DOJ) should issue joint guidance on the discipline of students with disabilities under IDEA and Section 504 that reconciles the obligation to provide a FAPE with the 10-day suspension rule[7] and focuses on how special education supports and services in the general education classroom

[7] 20 U.S.C. § 1415(k)(1)(B).

can support students who are at risk of academic failure and suspensions.

- Schools should develop data-driven early warning systems to identify students whose academic and behavioral issues put them at risk of suspensions and expulsions that lead to entry into the juvenile justice and criminal justice systems and refer these students for more intensive general or special education services and supports.
- ED and DOJ should bolster efforts to monitor and enforce the provision of FAPE to students with disabilities in the least restrictive environment.
- ED should issue guidance setting forth minimum substantive standards for the quality and delivery of special education and related services, particularly as they relate to behavioral supports.
- Federal and state enforcement activities must directly address race to remedy longstanding racial disparities in the placement and discipline of students with disabilities.
- ED should fund the development of systems for evaluating implicit racial and disability bias in schools where minorities are overrepresented in identification, discipline, or placement, and implement implicit bias training in enforcement agreements and compliance reviews.
- ED should take affirmative steps to enforce mandatory data collection and reporting requirements and ensure the validation of data submitted.
- Federal and state enforcement agencies should coordinate enforcement of disability rights laws and other civil rights laws such as Title VI of the Civil Rights Act of 1964 and bolster enforcement efforts on the specific issue of disproportionality in school discipline and juvenile justice referrals, including initiating litigation.

Conclusion

There is no question that the statistical picture of special education is bleak. But after its meeting of stakeholders, interviews with experts, and review of the research, NCD believes that IDEA and other related disability laws, with improved enforcement, can and should benefit at-risk students who are properly referred and served. In fact, the interventions and supports developed in special education are the key recommendations in the My Brother's Keeper Task Force report and other initiatives to curb the School-to-

Prison Pipeline in general education.[8] Special educators and the Office of Special Education and Rehabilitative Services (OSERS) should play a leading role in both special and general education reform. However, improved implementation of disability laws alone will not eliminate persistent racial disparities in special education. Enforcement activities must also address race head on to finally ameliorate the problem of disproportionality in special education.

SECTION 2: INTRODUCTION

A review of the literature on special education and students of color reveals a belief that special education is part of the problem, not part of the solution, to addressing the School-to-Prison Pipeline.[9] Rather than hailing IDEA as a proud descendant of the civil rights movement that preceded it, many view it as a threat to *Brown v. Board of Education*.[10] There is continuing fear of the label "disabled" because of the stigma attached to it.

This view is understandable given the dire statistics on educational outcomes and discipline. Students with disabilities are more than twice as likely to receive an out-of-school suspension (13%) than students without disabilities (6%).[11] IDEA students represent a quarter of students subjected to a school-related arrest, even though they are only 12 percent of the overall student population.[12] In 2011–2012, the national graduation rate for students with disabilities was just 61 percent, compared to 80 percent for all students.[13] In 2013, 75 percent of twelfth-grade students with disabilities scored "below

[8] My Brother's Keeper Task Force. "My Brother's Keeper Task Force Report to the President." May 2014. http://www.whitehouse.gov/sites/default/files/docs/053014_mbk_report.pdf

[9] Hing, Julianne. "Race, Disability and the School-to-Prison Pipeline." *Colorlines,* May 13, 2014, http://colorlines.com/archives/2014/05/race_disability_and_the_school_to_prison_pipeline.html.

[10] Erevelles, Nirmala. *Disability and difference in global contexts: Enabling a transformative body politic*. Palgrave Macmillan, 2011. ("Why do supporters of *Brown* not recognize how the assigned status of disability could serve as a mechanism for re-segregating students of color in otherwise desegregated schools?").

[11] Civil Rights Data Collection. Data Snapshot: School Discipline.

[12] Ibid.

[13] Stetser and Stillwell, "Public High School Four-Year On-Time Graduation Rates and Event Dropout Rates: School Years 2010–11 and 2011–12."

basic" on their National Assessment of Educational Progress (NAEP) math assessment, compared to 31 percent of nondisabled students.[14]

The numbers are even worse for students of color with disabilities. Twenty-seven percent of African American boys with disabilities and 19 percent of African American girls with disabilities received at least one out-of-school suspension in 2011–2012.[15] Students of color with disabilities remain disproportionately segregated from their peers without disabilities across all educational environments.[16] Most notably, African American students with disabilities represent 18.7 percent of the IDEA population, but 49.9 percent of IDEA students in correctional facilities.[17] Students of color also continue to be overrepresented and misrepresented in special education.[18]

What the literature and data fail to point out is that these negative outcomes are often the result of noncompliance with IDEA and other disability rights laws. Accordingly, NCD convened a stakeholder forum in conjunction with its quarterly meeting in Atlanta on October 6, 2014, to explore whether IDEA could be used effectively to address the School-to-Prison Pipeline. The questions posed to participants were:

> Does IDEA offer important tools to infuse better educational services for minority students with disabilities who are currently suspended or expelled? Can the proper implementation of IDEA help disrupt the School-to-Prison Pipeline for these students?

At the meeting, federal agency representatives, NCD members, and advocates from across the country with a broad array of expertise answered in the affirmative and explained how they are using IDEA in their daily practices to secure services and divert students from the Pipeline. While these stakeholders know that IDEA is not self-executing and that implementation is most often faulty, they feel that it is currently the best tool to infuse services to struggling students with disabilities. Instead of rejecting special education because of the stigma attached to "disability," NCD urges increased efforts to

---

[14] U.S. Department of Education. "2013 Mathematics and Reading: Grade 12 Assessments." *The Nation's Report Card*. http://www.nationsreportcard.gov/reading_math_g12_2013/# /reaching-proficient.

[15] Civil Rights Data Collection. Data Snapshot: School Discipline.

[16] U.S. Department of Education. *36th Annual Report to Congress on the Implementation of the Individuals with Disabilities Education Act*, 2014. http://www2.ed.gov/about/reports/ annual/osep/2014/parts-b-c/36th-idea-arc.pdf.

[17] IDEA Data Center. 2012 IDEA Part B Child Count and Educational Environments. https://ideadata.org/resource-library/#public-data.

[18] Ibid.

destigmatize disability in schools. Unfortunately, schools have too often reinforced the stigma through segregation and subpar curricula.[19]

NCD was also interested in how students of color with disabilities specifically could benefit from improved implementation of disability laws. Meeting participants explained that while consistent procedures, nonbiased assessments, proper behavioral plans and interventions, and academic supports would go a long way toward preventing arbitrary bias from seeping into IDEA implementation, enforcement and monitoring activities must still directly confront racial disparities caused by structural racism and implicit biases to maximize the potential of IDEA as a vehicle for breaking the School-to-Prison Pipeline.

NCD also learned how general and special education research advances and more expansive data collection and reporting requirements have allowed advocates to target specific problem areas for disability rights litigation and administrative advocacy. The following are recent examples of advocates using IDEA, Section 504, and the ADA as vehicles for instituting School-to-Prison Pipeline reforms:

- SWPBIS, RTI, restorative justice practices, and other programs instituted pursuant to successful Section 504 and ADA Title II federal administrative complaints have reduced suspensions and improved student reading levels, graduation rates, and other key measures;[20]
- Disability rights lawyers are increasingly bringing ADA Title II litigation to reform schools' delivery of special education and related services, including their systems for delivering mental health and behavioral services;[21] and
- Advocates have successfully used systemic IDEA state complaints to reform discriminatory school discipline policies[22] and special education delivery systems, including methods for providing

[19] Federal law dubs special education teachers "highly qualified" even if they are still working on their certification through an alternative training program like Teach for America. 20 U.S.C. § 1161f.

[20] Southern Poverty Law Center. "Palm Beach County Schools Reach Agreement with SPLC, Advocates to Reduce Exclusionary School Discipline." February 5, 2009. http://www.splcenter.org/get-informed/news/palm-beach-county-schools-reach-agreement-with-splc-advocates-to-reduce-exclusiona.

[21] Complaint, *S.S. v. Springfield Public Schools*, No. 14-30116 (D. Mass, Jun. 27, 2014). Available at: http://www.bazelon.org/portals/0/In%20Court/Current%20Cases/Current%20 Cases/Springfield%20MASS%20School%20System_Filed%2006271 4.pdf.

[22] Southern Poverty Law Center. "Calcasieu Parish Public School System." http://www.splcenter. org/get-informed/case-docket/calcasieu-parish-public-school-system.

individualized positive behavioral interventions and supports such as functional behavioral assessments (FBAs) and behavioral intervention plans (BIPs).[23]

In short, advocates now have a much firmer understanding of how to achieve the goal of providing effective and appropriate general and special education services to students with disabilities at risk of entering the School-to-Prison Pipeline. But greater enforcement of existing disability laws by relevant federal and state agencies is needed to ensure schools implement these research-based interventions with fidelity.

This report sets forth NCD's recommendations for federal, state, and local agencies and other key stakeholders on how to improve implementation of disability laws and address racial and ethnic disparities in special education.[24] NCD gathered the recommendations from testimony at the Atlanta meeting, follow-up interviews, and extensive research.

In agreement with them, NCD also incorporated many of the recommendations that came out of the November 20, 2014, Civil Rights Roundtable, a national meeting organized by the National Disability Rights Network to discuss intersectional approaches to reducing disproportionality in discipline and juvenile justice referrals.

---

[23] Advocates for Children. "Complaint Filed before the New York State Education Department by Advocates for Children of New York against the New York City Department of Education." http://www.advocatesforchildren.org/litigation/afc.

[24] The intent of the report is to question and explore how special education and the disability laws can be is part of the solution, instead of part of the problem to the School-to-Prison Pipeline. Because the report focuses on the entry points to the Pipeline, it does not address the education of students with disabilities currently in juvenile facilities. Two helpful resources on this important topic are: National Council on Disability, "Addressing the Needs of Youth with Disabilities in the Juvenile Justice System," and Office of Special Education and Rehabilitative Services (OSERS). "Dear Colleague Letter." December 5, 2014. http://www2.ed.gov/policy/gen/guid/correctional-education/idea-letter.pdf. Nor does the report address the over-representation of students of color in special education, as this important topic dominates the literature and discussions on the topic. For in-depth, historical explorations of the overrepresentation problem, read Artiles, Alfredo J., Elizabeth B. Kozleski, Stanley C. Trent, David Osher, and Alba Ortiz. "Justifying and explaining disproportionality, 1968–2008: A critique of underlying views of culture." *Exceptional Children* 76, no. 3 (2010): 279–299; and Cross, Christoper T., and M. Suzanne Donovan, eds. *Minority students in special and gifted education*. National Academies Press, 2002.

SECTION 3: THE INDIVIDUALS WITH DISABILITIES EDUCATION ACT (IDEA)

The legislative history of IDEA reveals Congress' intent to address discrimination on the basis of both disability and race/ethnicity. In a June 1975 report, the Senate Committee on Labor and Public Welfare noted that the proposed Act was more expansive than Section 504 because it included protections for "poor, minority, and bilingual children" in addition to students with disabilities.[25] The original bill contained language prohibiting schools from administering tests and evaluations used for the purpose of classification and placement of children with disabilities in a racially or culturally discriminatory manner.[26] Congress also drew inspiration from the 1972 case *Mills v. Board of Education*,[27] which guaranteed African American students with behavioral disabilities the right to a FAPE.

Four decades after the passage of the landmark IDEA, we have yet to fully realize the law's original nondiscriminatory purposes. The disproportionate discipline of all students with disabilities and particularly students of color with disabilities suggests a lack of access to appropriate special education and related services designed to address behavioral challenges through educational, not punitive, interventions. Furthermore, schools have used the disciplinary provisions Congress added during the last two reauthorizations of IDEA to circumvent educational interventions for behavior problems until after 10 days of suspension, after grave educational loss.[28] Compounding these failures is the presence of implicit racial and ethnic biases that influence disciplinary decision making and other special education processes.

NCD believes that administrative guidance would be the most effective method to improve IDEA implementation. In particular, the U.S. Department of Education (ED) must reconcile the obligation of schools to provide FAPE to students who have behavioral challenges with current abuses of IDEA disciplinary provisions. ED must then strictly monitor and enforce state education agency (SEA) and local education agency (LEA) compliance with

---

[25] S. Rep. No. 94-168 (1975).

[26] Education for All Handicapped Children Act, PL 94–142, 89 Stat 773 (1975).

[27] *Mills v. Bd. Of Educ. Of the Dist. of Columbia*, 348 F.Supp. 866 (1972).

[28] 10 days is "too long and creates significant barriers to reengagement, students' ability to keep pace with their peers, and other related problems." Morgan, E., Nina Salomon, Martha Plotkin, and Rebecca Cohen. *The School Discipline Consensus Report: Strategies from the Field to Keep Students Engaged in School and Out of the Juvenile Justice System.* New York: The Council of State Governments Justice Center, 2014. http://csgjusticecenter.org/wp-content/uploads/2014/06/The_School_Discipline_ Consensus_Report.pdf.

the FAPE and least restrictive environment (LRE) provisions of IDEA, including the requirements relating to positive behavioral interventions and supports, RTI, child find, and transition planning.

DISCIPLINE UNDER IDEA

Schools continue to exclude students with disabilities at disproportionate rates despite more than four decades of political and scholarly attention to this issue. Nationally, students with disabilities are more than twice as likely to receive an out-of-school suspension (13%) than students without disabilities (6%).[29] The statistics are even worse for students of color with disabilities. In 2009–2010, one out of every four (25%) African American children with disabilities in grades K–12 received at least one suspension.[30]

Out-of-School Suspension Rates by Race and Disability Status, 2009–2010[31]

Race	Suspension Rate for Disabled Students (%)	Suspension Rate for Nondisabled Students (%)
All	13	7
African American	25	16
Latino/Hispanic	12	7
Native American	11	8
White	9	4
Asian	3	2

Reducing these disparities is imperative. Frequent use of out-of-school suspensions has no academic benefit and is strongly associated with low achievement, a heightened risk for dropping out, and a greater likelihood of juvenile justice involvement.[32]

---

[29] Civil Rights Data Collection. Data Snapshot: School Discipline.

[30] Losen, Daniel J., and Jonathan Gillespie. "Opportunities suspended: The disparate impact of disciplinary exclusion from school." 2012. http://civilrightsproject.ucla.edu/resources/projects/center-for-civil-rights-remedies/school-to-prison-folder/federal-reports/upcoming-ccrr-research.

[31] Ibid.

[32] Losen, Daniel, Tia Martinez, and Jon Gillespie. "Suspended Education in California." 2012. http://civilrightsproject.ucla.edu/resources/projects/center-for-civil-rights-remedies/school-to-prison-folder/summary-reports/suspended-education-in-california/SuspendedEd-final3.pdf.

The Relationship between Discipline and FAPE

NCD believes that faithful implementation of IDEA and other disability rights laws guaranteeing a FAPE in the LRE would help reduce disproportionality in discipline and juvenile justice referrals. But in practice, the confusing IDEA disciplinary framework, particularly the provision allowing schools to remove students with disabilities up to 10 days, has been an impediment to proper IDEA implementation.

IDEA's "10-day rule" allows school personnel to

> remove a child with a disability who violates a code of student conduct from their current placement to an appropriate interim alternative educational setting, another setting, or suspension, for not more than 10 school days (to the extent such alternatives are applied to children without disabilities).[33]

Congress instituted the 10-day rule during the 1997 reauthorization, when lobbyists of the National School Boards Association and other organizations representing administrators and teachers urged that children with and without disabilities should be disciplined the same. The detailed and confusing compromise lawmakers reached with these groups maintained procedural protections for students with disabilities only after 10 days of suspensions in a school year.

IDEA defines a FAPE as "special education and related services that have been provided at public expense, under public supervision and direction, and without charge; meet the standards of the SEA; include an appropriate preschool, elementary school, or secondary school education in the state involved; and are provided in conformity with the individualized education program (IEP)."[34] Special education and related services must provide an education that is "specifically designed to meet the child's unique needs, supported by services that will permit him 'to benefit' from instruction."[35]

In practice, the 10-day rule has allowed schools to ignore their overarching obligation to provide a FAPE to students with disabilities. Schools have interpreted the 10-day rule as giving them 10 "free" removal days for each IDEA student—"free" in that the days can be used without an IEP team meeting, a BIP, an FBA, or any other service or support. This interpretation is

---

[33] 20 U.S.C. § 1415(k)(1)(B).

[34] 20 U.S.C. § 1401(9).

[35] *Cypress-Fairbanks Indep. Sch. Dist. v. Michael F.*, 118 F.3d 245, 247-248 (5th Cir. 1997), *cert. denied*, 522 U.S. 1047 (1998).

particularly harmful for students most likely to have behaviors that are manifestations of their disabilities.

Informational materials produced by private law firms representing school districts demonstrate this prevailing interpretation. The following excerpt is from a pamphlet titled "The Relationship Between Discipline and FAPE," created by a Texas-based law firm representing school districts:

> Schools have free use of up to 10 school days of short-term removals per school year without IDEA implications. The days can be used in any combination, quickly or slowly, although caution would warrant using the 10 "free" days judiciously over the school year, and avoiding multiple suspension days if at all possible.[36]

Under this interpretation of the 10-day rule, short-term suspensions are accepted behavioral tools schools can strategically spread out over the course of the school year. Schools have no incentive to intervene on behalf of struggling IDEA students until the eleventh day of removal. But the IDEA right to a FAPE is severely and often irrevocably compromised after 10 days of suspension. Moreover, the overwhelming majority of suspensions incurred by students with disabilities are for less than 10 days, often by design to avoid IDEA obligations.

This interpretation also contradicts Congress' intent for schools to proactively address behavior prior to the eleventh day of removal. Responding to a growing body of behavioral research, Congress added provisions in the 1997 amendments on the use of positive behavioral interventions and supports to specifically address the persistent disproportionate discipline of students with disabilities. As Senator Edward Kennedy stated at the time,

> [D]iscipline should never be used as an excuse to exclude or segregate children with disabilities because of the failure to design behavioral management plans, or the failure to provide support services and staff training.[37]

The key addition was a provision requiring the IEP team to "consider the use of positive behavioral interventions and supports" during the development, review, and revision of an IEP for a child "whose behavior impedes the child's

---

[36] Martin, Jose L. "The Relationship Between Discipline and FAPE." http://www.ksde.org/Portals/0/SES/legal/conf12/03b-DisciplineAndFAPE.pdf.

[37] 143 Cong. Rec. S4318 (daily ed. May 12, 1997) (statement of Sen. Edward Kennedy).

learning or that of others."[38] Congress also authorized SEAs to use IDEA professional development funds to "provide training in methods of . . . positive behavioral interventions and supports to improve student behavior in the classroom"[39] and encouraged implementation of these supports through grants.[40]

The main supports contemplated in the 1997 amendments were the FBA and the BIP, two research-based procedures for addressing behaviors that had gained favor among special education experts. An FBA is a systematic process of identifying the purpose and function of problem behaviors by investigating preexisting environmental factors that motivate problem behaviors.[41] Based on the foundation provided by an FBA, a BIP is a concrete plan of action for reducing problem behaviors, dictated by the particular needs of the student exhibiting the behaviors.[42]

If schools deliver FBAs, BIPs, and other related behavioral interventions with fidelity, they can change behavior before it leads to disciplinary action. Unfortunately, schools only utilize these interventions when a child is removed from his or her placement (i.e., suspended or expelled more than 10 days) and the offending conduct is determined to be a manifestation of the child's disability, in accordance with IDEA.[43]

Joint Guidance on the Discipline of Students with Disabilities

To curb these abuses of the IDEA 10-day Rule, the Departments of Education and Justice must issue policy guidance on the discipline of students with disabilities under IDEA and Section 504. To date, NCD,[44] My Brother's Keeper Taskforce,[45] and other stakeholders have called on the Departments to

[38] 20 U.S.C. § 1414(d)(3)-(4); 34 C.F.R. § 300.324(a)-(b).

[39] 20 U.S.C. §1454(a)(3)(B)(iii)(I).

[40] Grants can be used to: (1) Ensure that pre-service and in-service training, to general as well as special educators, include positive behavior interventions and supports (20 U.S.C. §1464 (a)(6)(D) and (f)(2)(A)(iv)(I)); (2) Develop and disseminate PBIS models for addressing conduct that impedes learning (20 U.S.C. §1464(b)(2)(H)); and (3) Provide training and joint training to the entire spectrum of school personnel in the use of whole school positive behavioral interventions and supports (20 U.S.C. §1483(1)(C & D)). Positive Behavioral Interventions and Supports. "PBIS and the Law." https://www.pbis.org/school/pbis-and-the-law.

[41] Zirkel, Perry A. "Case Law for Functional Behavior Assessments and Behavior Intervention Plans: An Empirical Analysis." *Seattle UL Rev.* 35 (2011): 175.

[42] Ibid.

[43] 20 U.S.C. § 1415(k)(1)(F).

[44] National Council on Disability to Secretary of Education Arne Duncan, February 14, 2014. http://www.ncd.gov/publications/2014/01402014/

[45] My Brother's Keeper Task Force. "My Brother's Keeper Task Force Report to the President," at 40.

issue IDEA guidance similar to their January 8, 2014, joint "Dear Colleague" Letter and Guidance Packet regarding public schools' obligation under Title VI of the Civil Rights Act to administer student discipline without discriminating on the basis of race, color, or national origin.[46]

IDEA discipline guidance must first and foremost clarify the meaning of the 10-day rule and reconcile it with the overarching obligation of SEAs and LEAs to provide a FAPE.[47] It should also clarify the obligations of LEAs that seek to order a change in placement of a child with a disability that would exceed 10 days, including their obligation to conduct manifestation determinations and provide educational services irrespective of whether the behavior is determined to be a manifestation of the child's disability.

The guidance should also clarify that the requirement to "consider" FBAs and BIPs is actually a requirement to provide behavioral interventions when necessary for a student to benefit from special education. Congress intended the word "consider" to require a review of behavioral issues at the IEP stage for a student "whose behavior impedes [his or her] learning or that of others."[48] The IEP team's consideration of a student whose behavior would or could result in suspensions should result in an intervention plan to address those behaviors. If the school addresses the behavior without an FBA or BIP, the school should be required to show that its approach is evidence based and effective. In any case, the Departments should make it clear that schools cannot use discipline instead of proactive and affirmative approaches to behavioral issues. The Departments should also clarify that the failure of an IEP team to "consider" the use of positive behavioral interventions and supports for a student whose behavior results in suspensions is a substantive, not procedural, violation of FAPE.

ED and DOJ must also clarify the obligation of LEAs to inform families of their disciplinary due process rights and to provide this information in their native language. Language barriers prevent many parents, guardians, and caretakers of English language learners (ELLs) from meaningful participation

---

[46] Although the Title VI guidance did not directly address disability discrimination, the Departments noted their particular concern over significant disparities in the discipline of students with disabilities and stated they were "developing resources to assist schools and support teachers in using appropriate discipline practices for students with disabilities." U.S. Departments of Education and Justice. "Dear Colleague Letter on the Nondiscriminatory Application of School Discipline." January 8, 2014. http://www2.ed.gov/about/ offices/ list/ocr/letters/colleague-201401-title-vi.html.

[47] The most obvious solution would be to amend IDEA to eliminate the 10 "free" days of suspension. However, NCD does not believe that this is a good time to open IDEA for revisions in the disciplinary provisions.

[48] 34 C.F.R. § 300.324(a)(2).

in the complicated IDEA discipline process, and schools are often unable or unwilling to provide necessary translation and interpretation services. As a result, many families agree to forgo IDEA due process procedures and accept "voluntary transfers" to more restrictive alternative and continuation schools. This is an unacceptable, yet very common, form of discipline for ELLs.

Finally, IDEA guidance should clarify the meaning of the phrase "to the extent" contained in the language of the 10-day rule. The provision states that schools may remove a student with a disability for up to 10 days "to the extent such alternatives are applied to children without disabilities."[49] So long as there is overrepresentation of students with disabilities in suspension data, discipline is not being used "to the extent" it is applied to students without disabilities. Disproportionate suspensions of students with disabilities should trigger an examination of the eligibility of the disciplined students as well as the quality of assessments, behavior plans, IEPs, and placements by enforcing agencies.

Recommendation:

3.1. Similar to their joint January 2014 Title VI guidance, ED and DOJ should issue a "Dear Colleague" Letter and policy guidance on the discipline of students with disabilities under IDEA and Section 504. The guidance should:

- Reconcile the obligation to provide a FAPE with the 10-day rule by clarifying the obligation of IEP Teams to proactively consider the use of positive behavioral interventions and support prior to the eleventh day of removal;
- Clarify that the failure of an IEP team to "consider" the use of positive behavioral interventions and supports for a student whose behavior results in suspensions is a substantive, not procedural violation of FAPE;
- Clarify the obligations of an LEA when it seeks to order a change in placement that would exceed 10 school days, including the obligation to perform manifestation determinations;
- Describe standards for the special education, related services, and positive behavior interventions and supports (such as FBAs and BIPs) needed for students with behavioral challenges to receive a FAPE;

[49] 20 U.S.C. § 1415(k)(1)(B).

- Clarify the obligations of LEAs to inform families of their IDEA due process rights, including their rights during the complicated IDEA disciplinary process, and to translate this information into families' native language;
- Clarify the illegality of "voluntary transfer" and other circumventions of IDEA disciplinary processes that disproportionately affect parents, guardians, and caretakers of ELLs; and
- Clarify the meaning of the phrase "to the extent such alternatives are applied to children without disabilities" contained in the language of the 10-day rule.

Section 504 Shortened School Day Guidance

Related to the abuse of IDEA disciplinary provisions is the fact that schools remove students with disabilities from classroom instruction by informal means as a way to circumvent the 10-day rule. This occurs through the use of shortened school days (e.g., repeated "sent homes " or changes to the IEP or Section 504 plan that provide the child less than a full school day), forced withdrawals from school, compulsory transfers to inadequate alternative programs or very limited homebound instruction, lengthy stays in seclusion rooms, and other methods. These removals do not count toward the 10-day threshold triggering IDEA safeguards despite the fact they often add up to much more than 10 days out of school.

National Disability Rights Network (NDRN) currently has a national project to draw attention to the issue of informal removals from school. NDRN believes that informal removals of students with disabilities have increased due to the increased scrutiny on formal removals such as suspension and expulsions. In May 2014, NDRN submitted a letter to ED's Office for Civil Rights (OCR) formally asking the agency to address this hidden epidemic through policy guidance that incorporates the following Shortened School Day Principles:

1) **Affirm the Right of All Students to a Full School Day.** This principle is consistent with the Section 504 regulations at 34 C.F.R. Part 104.
2) **Define Shortened School Day.** OCR should define "Shortened school day" as "any day in which a student with a disability attends school for less time than students without disabilities."
3) **Shortened School Days and Disciplinary Processes.** OCR should explain that shortened school days that have not occurred pursuant to

Section 504, IDEA, or general education disciplinary procedures are potentially discriminatory.

4) **"Significant or Material Loss."** OCR should provide examples of a "significant or material loss" needed to signify a violation of Section 504.
5) **Review Relevant Regulatory Requirements.** OCR should clarify the obligation of LEAs under Section 504 to provide a FAPE in the LRE to all students with disabilities, including students with behavioral issues.
6) **Discuss Budgetary Constraints**. OCR should clarify that budgetary constraints do not warrant a school giving a student a shorter school day.
7) **"Earning" a Full Day.** OCR should clarify that behavioral incentives cannot include earning educational services or time in school.
8) **"An Hour is an Hour."** There is no legal authority to support the argument that an hour of homebound, one-on-one tutoring is worth a certain number of hours of in-class time.[50]
9) **A Need for Closer Analysis.** When a school proposes a shortened day for behavioral reasons, it should review the student's IEP or 504 plan to see whether he or she is receiving proper services and supports.
10) **Data and Funding.** OCR should review how shortened school days are recorded for federal data collection purposes to ensure that data collection systems do not indirectly encourage the use of shortened school days. Similarly, OCR should encourage SEAs to review whether state funding formulae encourage homebound or shortened day programming by providing full reimbursement for partial days of school.

Each principle is consistent with existing Section 504 regulations, policy statements, and principles enunciated in OCR decisions. Therefore, there is no need for amendments to Section 504 or its implementing regulations.

---

[50] In *Limestone County (AL) School District*, 114 LRP 48956 (OCR 06/10/14), OCR determined that the LEA violated 504 by setting universal rules governing who was eligible for the homebound services and limiting students to three hours of instruction per week. ED-OCR explained that, under Section 504 and Title II, a district must provide students with disabilities with the regular or special education and related aids and services that meet their needs as adequately as the needs of nondisabled students are met.

Recommendation:

3.2. ED-OCR should issue guidance that addresses shortened school days and other informal means of removals and clarify that they are illegal when used to circumvent statutory and regulatory protections. The guidance should incorporate each of NDRN's Shortened School Day Principles.

FAPE Enforcement

Once ED and DOJ clarify IDEA, Section 504, and ADA obligations of SEAs and LEAs, they must then vigorously monitor and enforce the provision of FAPE to students who have behavioral challenges.

Indicators 4A and 4B: Suspension/Expulsion

IDEA requires the federal Office of Special Education Programs (OSEP) to monitor SEAs, and SEAs to monitor LEAs, using quantifiable indicators that measure either compliance with specific statutory or regulatory provisions of IDEA (compliance indicators) or results and outcomes for children with disabilities and their families (results indicators).[51] The 20 Part B indicators created by OSEP target the following priority areas: (A) provision of a free appropriate public education in the least restrictive environment; (B) state exercise of general supervisory authority, including child find, effective monitoring, the use of resolution sessions, mediation, voluntary binding arbitration, and a system of transition services; and (C) disproportionate representation of racial and ethnic groups in special education and related services, to the extent the representation is the result of inappropriate identification.[52]

This current monitoring system is not equipped to remedy the abuses of the IDEA 10-day rule and ensure the provision of FAPE to students suspended less than 10 days.[53] SEAs monitor LEA compliance with IDEA disciplinary provisions through OSEP Indicators 4A and 4B, which only measure the rates of suspensions and expulsions of children with disabilities (including, in the case of 4B, data disaggregated by race and ethnicity) for greater than 10 days. Advocates have long urged OSEP to expand the scope of Indicators 4A and

---

[51] 20 U.S.C. § 1416(a)(3); 34 C.F.R. § 300.600(c).
[52] Ibid.
[53] *See* Section 3, *supra*.

4B to include suspensions of less than 10 days, especially since the Section 618 discipline data should be readily available.

A recent decision in the IDEA class action case *Emma C. v. Eastin*[54] validated these criticisms of Indicators 4A and 4B. In *Emma C.*, the plaintiffs challenged the adequacy of the California Department of Education's (CDE) state-level monitoring system, arguing, *inter alia*, that CDE's exclusive use of Indicator 4A and 4B failed to connect suspensions of any length to potential child find and FAPE violations. Plaintiffs further argued that IDEA requires an individualized record review of students suspended or expelled to monitor whether a denial of a FAPE and/or behavior related to students' disabilities has caused the high rates of suspension.

The Court Monitor agreed in his January 9, 2014, report and ordered CDE to engage in corrective action steps "reasonably calculated to ensure that students with disabilities subjected to disciplinary removals for fewer than 10 days are receiving a FAPE, including any positive behavior supports necessary for them to receive FAPE."[55] The Court Monitor's findings and Judge Thelton Henderson's subsequent order approving these findings underscore the serious deficiencies in the current discipline monitoring model.[56]

Recommendation:

3.3. OSEP should expand the scope of OSEP Indicators 4A and 4B to include suspensions of less than 10 days and to require a record review to determine if LEAs should have addressed the behavior in the IEP or failed to deliver the IEP services with fidelity. This change would help curb abuses of the IDEA 10-day rule and ensure the provision of FAPE to students suspended less than 10 days. Congress would not have to amend IDEA since Section 618 already requires SEAs to collect data on suspensions of less than 10 days.[57]

Early Intervention Systems: FAPE Triggers and Response to Intervention

LEAs should develop protocols to ensure they are not punishing students with IEPs for problematic behaviors caused by educational deficiencies. An

---

[54] *Emma C. v. Eastin*, No. 96–cv–04179–TEH (N.D. Cal. 1996).

[55] The Court Monitor's Report is on file with the authors.

[56] *Emma C. v. Eastin*, 2014 WL 2989946 (N.D. Cal., July 2, 2014).

[57] Of course, participants acknowledged that the best solution would be to repeal the 10 day rule in the statute, but are not confident that Congress would do so.

example would be for a short-term suspension to trigger a review of a student's IEP to ensure it is reasonably calculated to provide FAPE. A review of a suspended student's records will likely show a problem with instruction or other underlying problems that schools cannot remedy through exclusionary discipline. These periodic reviews would also give the IEP team an opportunity to consider or modify the use of FBAs, BIPs, and other positive behavioral interventions and supports to ensure the student stays in school.

One such protocol is the Behavioral Support Continuum created by Fluency Plus, Inc. for Jackson Public Schools of Jackson, Mississippi. The continuum calls for procedural safeguards for reviewing and revising students IEPs and BIPs following removals from school of two, four, six, and 10 days, respectively, for any disciplinary reason.[58] The Council of State Governments called for a similar system in their influential 2014 School Discipline Consensus Report and included a thorough review of examples currently in place across the country.[59]

For students without IEPs, SEAs and LEAs should implement RTI, a school-wide, multi-step process of providing academic and behavioral supports and interventions.[60] While there are different RTI frameworks, experts agree that the core features of an RTI model are: (1) students receive high-quality, research-based instruction in their general education setting; (2) continuous monitoring of student performance; (3) all students are screened for academic and behavioral problems; and (4) multiple levels (tiers) of instruction that are progressively more intense, based on the student's response to instruction.[61] Rather than wait years for a student to fail, RTI assumes that if students who are identified by the universal screening process continue to demonstrate an inadequate response to a sequence of intensified, evidenced-based behavior supports, then that student can and should be given more intensive intervention assistance including, but not limited to, special education and related services.[62]

---

[58] Jackson (MS) Public Schools. "Support Services/Child Find." http://www.jackson.k12.ms.us/content.aspx?url=/page/eessupport.

[59] Morgan, Salomon, Plotkin, and Cohen. *The School Discipline Consensus Report: Strategies from the Field to Keep Students Engaged in School and Out of the Juvenile Justice System.*

[60] RTI Action Network. "What Is RTI?" http://rtinetwork.org/learn/what/whatisrti.

[61] Office of Special Education Programs. "Policy Memorandum 11-07." January 2011. https://www2.ed.gov/policy/speced/guid/idea/memosdcltrs/osep11-07rtimemo.pdf.

[62] Gresham, Frank M. "Response to Intervention and Emotional and Behavioral Disorders Best Practices in Assessment for Intervention." *Assessment for Effective Intervention* 32, no. 4 (2007): 214-222.

ED and many SEAs strongly support LEA implementation of RTI strategies. But for RTI to reach its potential as a School-to-Prison Pipeline reform, ED and SEAs must oversee LEA RTI implementation closely as part of their IDEA monitoring and enforcement responsibilities to ensure that schools are not violating their IDEA child find requirements by using RTI to deny or delay special education assessments.[63]

Recommendations:

3.4. Schools should develop data-driven early warning systems to identify students at risk of retention, dropping out, or entry into the juvenile justice system. Under these systems, schools would refer students with short-term suspension, poor grades, and chronic absenteeism for more intensive general education or special education services. Recommended systems include school-wide RTI as well as FAPE trigger systems specifically for students receiving services under IDEA Parts B or C. Schools implementing these frameworks must pay specific attention to race and ethnicity data.[64]

3.5. ED should require schools with certain characteristics (e.g., racial disproportionality in rates of identification or in discipline, high use of placements segregated by race or by disability), to use federal Coordinated Early Intervening Services (CEIS) to implement evidence-based approaches to RTI.

3.6. ED and SEAs must make RTI pilot programs a priority and continue to utilize RTI and other early intervention systems as corrective actions in complaints brought pursuant to IDEA, Section 504, ADA, and Title VI.

3.7. ED and SEAs must monitor LEA implementation of RTI, including as a means of assessing special education eligibility for some students (e.g., SLD under 20 U.S.C. § 1414(b)(6)(B)), as part of their IDEA monitoring and enforcement responsibilities to ensure schools are not violating their IDEA child find requirements by using RTI to deny or delay special education assessments.

---

[63] Office of Special Education Programs. "Policy Memorandum 11-07." ("States and LEAs have an obligation to ensure that evaluations of children suspected of having a disability are not delayed or denied because of an RTI strategy").

[64] See the discussion on Race-Conscious Positive Behavioral Interventions and Supports in Section 4, *supra.*

FAPE Enforcement Actions

The Departments of Education and Justice could significantly improve SEA and LEA provision of FAPE by bringing or intervening in School-to-Prison Pipeline litigation and investigations. NCD believes that one cannot separate suspensions from the provision of FAPE. If schools provided FAPE to students with disabilities, suspensions would be the exception rather than the rule to deal with nonconforming behavior. Failing grades and lack of educational success can lead to behaviors that result in suspension. If a student served under IDEA or Section 504 is suspended frequently, the cause may well lie in the lack of supports or services delivered with fidelity.

Dealing with the suspension issue without looking at the underlining cause is the ultimate example of dealing with the symptoms rather than the disease. The disease is an educational system focused on paper compliance and that does not value all students equally or have proper accountability standards. ED- or DOJ-ordered remedies should not focus solely on discipline but on the underlying failure of schools to provide FAPE to students subject to punitive discipline.[65]

Recommendation:

3.8. ED and DOJ should bolster their efforts to enforce the provision of FAPE to students with disabilities by:

- Bringing enforcement actions or intervening in private-party lawsuits regarding: (1) Failure to provide FAPE including academic and behavioral supports in the general education classroom (2) the lack of educational equity in some or all of a school district's programs; (3) attempts to institute evidence-based programs that enhance or expand services to at-risk youth (e.g., RTI); (4) unnecessary segregation of students with disabilities; and (5) disproportionate suspensions and expulsions.
- Filing statements of interest in private lawsuits that take helpful positions on the law, specifically drawing attention to the improper use of the "10-day rule" to eviscerate the requirement for behavioral interventions at the IEP stage; and

[65] There is a particular need for formal Federal Government enforcement of FAPE in charter schools. Despite being subject to IDEA, Section 504, and ADA, charter schools often deny admission to students with disabilities and ELLS, citing them as "bad fits" or claiming they do not serve these populations.

- Ensuring that charter schools recruit, enroll, support, and provide opportunities for students with disabilities and ELLs to benefit and succeed.

School-Based Mental Health and Behavioral-Related Services

The quality and delivery of school-based mental health and behavioral-related services must improve for IDEA to realize its potential as a vehicle for breaking the School-to-Prison Pipeline. IDEA regulations define the related services available to students under the law[66] but do not give schools guidance on what these services must look like in practice. The lack of quality standards coupled with the inadequacy of monitoring from state and federal oversight agencies has allowed schools to "comply" with IDEA while providing ineffective services. OSERS could effectively "raise the bar" regarding what it means to receive a FAPE by issuing administrative guidance articulating standards for school-based mental health and behavioral-related services and then strictly enforcing these standards.

Mental Health Services

Among the special education and related services available to eligible students under IDEA to ensure a FAPE are school-based mental health services.[67] When delivered appropriately, these services enable students with behavioral, emotional, and mental health needs to learn in general education classrooms, progress from grade to grade, and earn high school diplomas.

Advocates are now turning to ADA and Section 504 to reform systems for delivering school-based mental health and behavior services. A recent example is the federal class action lawsuit *S.S. v. Springfield Public Schools*[68] filed in June 2014. The *S.S.* complaint alleges that the public schools of Springfield, Massachusetts, violate Title II of the ADA by placing children with mental health needs in "public day schools," where they are subjected to dangerous physical restraints, forced isolation in padded rooms, and repeated arrests and suspensions for minor offenses.[69] To contrast the district's practices, the

[66] 34 C.F.R. § 300.34(c).

[67] In many states, these IDEA services are medically necessary under the Early and Periodic Screening, Diagnostic and Treatment (EPSDT) benefit of the Medicaid Act and are reimbursable for students enrolled in Medicaid. 42 U.S.C. §§ 1396a and 1396d.

[68] Complaint, *S.S. v. Springfield Public Schools*, No. 14-30116 (D. Mass, Jun. 27, 2014).

[69] Ibid.

complaint describes professional standards for delivering quality school-based mental health services.[70]

Courts have held that ADA and Section 504 protections are independent of, and not coextensive with, the basic floor of access to education guaranteed by IDEA under the Supreme Court's decision in *Bd. of Educ. of Hendrick Hudson Cent. Sch. Dist. v. Rowley*.[71] ED and DOJ have affirmed this interpretation through involvement in private suits such as *S.S.*[72] and joint guidance explaining that schools may have to provide services under ADA and Section 504 that are not required under IDEA.[73] The continued support of the ED and DOJ in efforts to use ADA and Section 504 to improve the quality and delivery of special education and related services is essential to achieving School-to-Prison Pipeline reform.

Recommendations:

3.9. OSEP should issue a guidance document explaining school districts' obligation under IDEA to provide FAPE to students with disabilities exhibiting problematic behaviors. This guidance should describe the special education and related services schools should provide to these students to ensure FAPE, including:

- Standards for school-based mental health and behavior services. As described in the *S.S. v. Springfield Public Schools* complaint, professionals agree that school-based mental health and behavior services should include: (a) a comprehensive assessment, including determination of the purpose and triggers for the child's behavior; (b) a school-based intervention plan that relies on positive support, social

[70] The *S.S.* complaint states that the following services are necessary to afford children with significant emotional disturbance "equal educational opportunity and the opportunity to be educated in neighborhood schools alongside their peers without disabilities": (a) a comprehensive assessment, including determination of the purpose and triggers for the child's behavior; (b) a school-based intervention plan that relies on positive support, social skills training, a care coordinator, and adjustments as needed to curriculum or schedules; (c) training for school staff and parents in implementing the plan; and (d) coordination with non-school providers involved with the child. Complaint, *S.S. v. Springfield Public Schools*, No. 14-30116 (D. Mass, Jun. 27, 2014).

[71] *See, e.g., K.M. v. Tustin Unified Sch. Dist.*, 725 F.3d 1088 (9th Cir. 2013).

[72] Statement of Interest of the United States of America, *S.S. v. Springfield Public Schools*, No. 14-30116 (D. Mass, Aug. 27, 2014).

[73] U.S. Departments of Education and Justice. "Dear Colleague Letter." November 12, 2014. http://www2.ed.gov/about/offices/list/ocr/letters/colleague-effective-communication-201411.pdf.

skills training, a care coordinator, and adjustments as needed to curriculum or schedules; (c) training for school staff and families in implementing the plan; and (d) coordination with nonschool providers involved with the child.

3.10. ED, SEAs, and LEAs should increase technical assistance and training on the substantive and procedural requirements for school-based mental health and behavior services. Oversight agencies must review the quality and delivery of these services whenever a district has an excessive or disproportionate use of discipline.

3.11. ED and the DOJ should continue administrative activities that support advocacy efforts to use ADA and Section 504 to improve the quality and delivery of special education and related services.

Barriers to Accessing Appropriate FBAs and BIPs

Although research continues to prove the efficacy of appropriate FBAs and BIPs in addressing problematic behaviors,[74] schools rarely use these interventions or implement them with fidelity. In practice, schools ignore the requirement to "consider" such supports in the IEP meeting or deal with it in a cursory manner. As discussed earlier, LEAs have no incentive to provide these interventions until they are required to do so by IDEA safeguards for students incurring long-term removals.[75]

Case law, state special education laws, and federal administrative guidance have only served to maintain this status quo. Predictably, administrative law judges (ALJs) and federal judges have interpreted the term "consider" in the IEP provisions as not requiring access to an FBA or BIP.[76] Some courts have further limited access by interpreting failures to provide these supports as procedural violations. This is a crucial distinction because a procedural violation is subject to the defense-friendly, harmless-error approach to FAPE.[77]

---

[74] National Council on Disability, "National Disability Policy: A Progress Report." 2014. http://www.ncd.gov/progress_reports/10312014.

[75] See Discussion of IDEA 10-day rule, *supra.*

[76] Zirkel. "Case Law for Functional Behavior Assessments and Behavior Intervention Plans: An Empirical Analysis."

[77] Professor Zirkel recommended determining access to FBAs and BIPs via the established IDEA standard for "related services." According to Professor Zirkel, this standard is preferable to the weak mandate to "consider" such supports because courts and ALJs will ask whether access to FBAs and BIPs is required to "assist a child with a disability to benefit from special education[.]" Moreover, the broad definition of related services in IDEA is sufficiently flexible to cover FBAs and BIPs.

States are also moving away from more expansive FBA and BIP standards. In July 2013, California—which previously had the most expansive FBA and BIP requirements in the country—repealed its regulations regarding the use of behavioral interventions in favor of the baseline standards articulated in IDEA and its implementing regulations.[78] The repeal coincided with the release of data showing that the state suspended students with disabilities at more than twice the rate of students without disabilities (13.4% to 6.4%) in 2009–2010, including a staggering 28 percent of all African American students with disabilities.[79]

Federal administrative guidance is similarly limiting. Since 1997, OSEP and OSERS have consistently stated that IDEA does not "require" an FBA for cumulative removals of less than 10 days in a school year, but that IEP teams "could" proactively conduct an FBA to address misconduct when it first appears.[80] Aside from this straightforward interpretation of the statute and its regulations, the agencies have not called for broader access to FBAs and BIPs.[81]

Even when students do receive FBAs and BIPs, these interventions are often inadequate and poorly implemented. LEAs rarely conduct FBAs consistent with professional norms.[82] Many FBAs involve nothing more than a record review, and are often boiler-plate and not individualized or based on ongoing data.[83] These cursory assessments provide little useful information for the IEP team to use in crafting behavioral interventions. Moreover, LEAs rarely perform FBAs before drafting BIPs despite the fact special education experts regard an FBA as inseparable from an effective BIP.[84] Without the baseline data an FBA provides, students receive ineffective, cookie-cutter

---

78 California Assembly Bill No. 86 (2013). Available at: http://leginfo.legislature.ca.gov/faces/billNavClient.xhtml?bill_id=201320140AB86.

79 Losen, Martinez, and Gillespie. "Suspended Education in California."

80 Office of Special Education Programs. "Policy Memorandum No. 97-7." September 19, 1997. https://www2.ed.gov/policy/speced/leg/idea/97-7.pdf.

81 IDEA Regulations Commentary, 71 Fed. Reg. 46,683 (Aug. 14, 2006).

82 Experts generally recommend that FBAs include: (1) operational definitions of problem behaviors; (2) descriptions of the assessment conditions that may reliably predict the occurrence and nonoccurrence of problem behaviors; (3) descriptions of the consequence events that maintain problem behaviors; (4) direct observation of the problem behaviors across the assessment conditions; and (5) a BIP based on the analysis of this information. Zirkel. "Case Law for Functional Behavior Assessments and Behavior Intervention Plans: An Empirical Analysis."

83 A DREDF client received a BIP that included inappropriate interventions such as, "Student will stop bringing candy to school"; "Student will ask himself, 'Am I paying attention?'"; and "Student will obey all school rules." The BIP is on file with DREDF.

84 Ibid.

BIPs that fail to reduce problem behaviors. Advocates have been unable to contest this practice because courts have consistently held that IDEA does not require an FBA prior to a BIP.[85]

Far too often, BIPs are sloppily written and poorly implemented. IDEA does not provide BIP standards, but in 2001 an Iowa ALJ created a four-pronged appropriateness test for BIPs that ALJs in other jurisdictions quickly adopted. Under this test, BIPs must:

I. Be based on assessment data;
II. Be individualized to meet the child's needs;
III. Include positive behavioral change strategies; and
IV. Be consistently implemented as planned and its effects monitored.[86]

Despite the popularity of this test, the Seventh Circuit later rejected it in *Alex R. v. Forrestville Valley Community School District*[87] due to the lack of specific substantive requirements for BIPs in IDEA or its regulations:

> Although we may interpret a statute and its implementing regulations, we may not create out of whole cloth substantive provisions for the behavioral intervention plan contemplated by [IDEA]. In short, the District's [BIP] could not have fallen short of substantive criteria that did not exist, and so we conclude as a matter of law that it was not substantively invalid under the IDEA.[88]

Since 1997, OSEP has issued several guidance documents encouraging schools to adhere to best practices,[89] but must increase monitoring and enforcement especially in the face of excessive suspensions and expulsions. LEAs must also avail themselves of the myriad professional development resources available to them, including OSEP's Technical Assistance Center on Positive Behavioral Interventions and Supports.[90]

---

[85] *See, e.g., R.P. ex rel. R.P. v. Alamo Heights Independent Sch. Dist.*, 703 F.3d 801, 813 (5th Cir. 2012).

[86] *Mason Cty. Cmty. Sch. Dist.* 36 IDELR ¶ 50 (Iowa 2001).

[87] *Alex R. v. Forrestville Valley Community School District*, 375 F.3d 603, 615 (7th Cir. 2004).

[88] Ibid.

[89] Office of Special Education Programs. "Behavior Assessment and Behavior Intervention Plans." November 1998. http://files.eric.ed.gov/fulltext/ED429420.pdf.

[90] Office of Special Education Programs. *Positive Behavioral Interventions and Supports.* www.pbis.org.

Recommendations:

3.12. In addition to school-based mental health and behavior services, OSERS guidance should describe standards for FBAs and BIPs, including:

- The minimal substantive components of an FBA;
- When to conduct an FBA prior to crafting a BIP; and
- The minimal substantive components of a BIP.

3.13. IEP teams must follow Congress' intent to proactively "consider" behavior through the use of FBAs, BIPs, and other individualized positive behavior interventions and supports at the IEP stage.

3.14. ED, SEAs, and LEAs should increase technical assistance and training on the substantive and procedural requirements for FBAs and BIPs.

3.15. ED and SEAs should increase enforcement and monitoring of preventative behavioral interventions in the face of excessive suspensions and expulsions.

Least Restrictive Environment and the Integration Mandate

Perhaps the biggest contributor to the poor reputation of IDEA and special education is the widespread belief that special education is a place where students are sent, never to return to general education. This segregation is a cause for shame and taunting by other students. The harshest critics of IDEA see it as another way to segregate students with disabilities post *Brown*.[91] The disproportionate segregation of disabled students of color feeds this belief. The federal agencies charged with special education and civil rights enforcement must develop a robust accountability and monitoring strategy on segregation if special education is ever to be a viable alternative for students of color.

[91] Erevelles, Nirmala. *Disability and difference in global contexts: Enabling a transformative body politic*. Palgrave Macmillan, 2011. ("Why do supporters of *Brown* not recognize how the assigned status of disability could serve as a mechanism for re-segregating students of color in otherwise desegregated schools?").

Inclusion/Integration Mandates

IDEA has a strong integration mandate that has yet to be fully realized, even 40 years after its passage. IDEA requires states to ensure that every student with a disability is educated in the LRE to the "maximum extent appropriate."[92] This means that the removal of a student with a disability may only occur "when the nature or severity of the disability of a child is such that education in regular classes with the use of supplementary aids and services cannot be achieved satisfactorily."[93] Similarly, Title II of the ADA includes an "integration mandate" that requires public entities to "administer services, programs, and activities in the most integrated setting appropriate to the needs of qualified individuals with disabilities."[94]

Government enforcement of the respective inclusion and integration requirements of IDEA, Section 504, and ADA, performed in conjunction with FAPE enforcement, is essential in breaking the School-to-Prison Pipeline. The overall inclusion of students with disabilities in the general education classroom has increased over the last decade,[95] but current statistics show that enforcement activities have not adequately targeted students with disabilities at risk of entering the School-to-Prison Pipeline. Many students with disabilities who could be educated in regular classes with behavioral interventions remain needlessly segregated in classrooms where they are more likely to receive inferior services and are subjected to physical restraints, forced seclusion, and repeated arrests and suspensions.[96] Students placed in segregated settings also have far worse educational outcomes than those who are mainstreamed.[97]

As shown by the most recent IDEA Section 618 data, students of color with disabilities in particular have not benefitted from increased inclusion:

[92] 20 U.S.C. § 1412(a)(5)(A).

[93] 20 U.S.C. § 1412(a)(5)(A).

[94] 28 C.F.R. § 35.130.

[95] The percentage of students with disabilities educated inside the regular class 80 percent or more of the day has increased from 49.9 percent in 2003 to 61.5 percent in 2012. U.S. Department of Education. *36th Annual Report to Congress on the Implementation of the Individuals with Disabilities Education Act*, 2014.

[96] Currently, students served by IDEA represent 12 percent of the student population but 58 percent of those placed in seclusion, 75 percent of those physically restrained, and 25 percent of those arrested at school. Civil Rights Data Collection. Data Snapshot: School Discipline.

[97] National Council on Disability, "National Disability Policy: A Progress Report," 2011.

Percentage of Students Ages 6 through 21 Served Under IDEA, Part B, Within Racial/Ethnic Groups, By Educational Environment: Fall 2012[98]

	Regular school: 80% or more	Regular school: 40–79%	Regular school: Less than 40%	Other Environments
All Students	61.5	19.5	13.8	5.2
American Indian or Alaska Native	62.6	23.9	10.6	2.9
Asian	56.6	16.7	21.1	5.7
Black or African American	55.6	20.4	17.9	6.1
Hispanic/Latino	60.1	19.7	16.3	3.9
Native Hawaiian or Other Pacific Islander	53.9	27.4	15.2	3.4
White	64.5	19.0	10.9	5.6
Two or More Races	63.3	19.3	13.0	4.4

It is clear from these figures that LRE/integration enforcement must target racial disparities to break the School-to-Prison Pipeline. Current federal and state enforcement systems do not directly address race despite the availability of placement data disaggregated by race.[99] For example, compliance with the LRE requirements is a priority area for federal monitoring and enforcement,[100] but OSEP Indicator 5 only measures an LEA's overall percentage of children with IEPs served in various placements. It does not require LEAs to meet any race-related benchmarks.

The separate IDEA significant disproportionality framework[101] requires SEAs to monitor significant disproportionality based on race and ethnicity in the placement of children with disabilities, but SEAs often set the bar so high that few if any LEAs are ever identified.[102] OSERS received over 80 comments in response to its June 2014 RFI on significant disproportionality but had not issued a formal response as of April 1, 2015. OSERS must ensure

[98] U.S. Department of Education. *36th Annual Report to Congress on the Implementation of the Individuals with Disabilities Education Act*, 2014.

[99] 20 U.S.C. § 1418(a)(1)(A)

[100] 20 U.S.C. § 1416(a)(3)(A); 34 C.F.R. § 300.646(d)(1).

[101] 20 U.S.C. § 1418(d); 34 C.F.R. § 300.600.

[102] Request for Information on Addressing Significant Disproportionality Under Section 618(d) of the Individuals With Disabilities Education Act (IDEA), 79 Fed. Reg. 35,154 (2014). http://www.gpo.gov/fdsys/pkg/FR-2014-06-19/pdf/2014-14388.pdf.

that changes to the significant disproportionality framework effectively address racial disparities in special education placement.

The segregation of students of color with behavioral issues should also trigger an investigation into whether schools use segregated special education classrooms as a dumping ground for students that schools could serve in the general education classroom with RTI or IDEA services. There is a correlation between segregation and the tremendous overrepresentation of students of color in special education. The premise of challenges to overrepresentation of students of color in special education is that schools use special education to get “problem” students out of the general education classroom, regardless of whether the child has a disability or whether the segregated special education placement is designed to address those problems. By uncovering instances of improper segregation of students of color, these investigations could curb the overrepresentation of students of color in special education while also ensuring that students who do need services will receive them in the general education classroom.

Recommendations:

3.16. The Federal Government and SEAs must increase LRE/integration enforcement to ensure that schools do not place students of color in more restrictive settings instead of providing general education interventions. For example, ED and DOJ should bring formal enforcement actions or intervene in private party lawsuits regarding the unnecessary segregation of students with disabilities.[103]

3.17. Federal and state monitoring activities must directly address race to remedy longstanding racial disparities in the placement of students with disabilities. OSEP should amend Indicator 5 to include compliance benchmarks to ensure LEAs are not disproportionately segregating students of color with disabilities. OSERS should enforce the requirement of SEAs to address significant disproportionality in the placement of children with disabilities in particular educational settings. The current system is opaque and does not reflect the glaring racial disparities in the placement of students with disabilities.

3.18. LEAs should provide behavioral services and supports to students with disabilities in the general education classroom. Too often,

[103] The rise of disability-only charter schools is a recent example of a potential circumvention of the IDEA LRE mandate.

schools only deliver these services in more restrictive settings. Federal and state enforcement should include a review of where schools are providing behavioral services and if parents are aware that students do not have to be segregated to receive such services. Many parents are currently unaware that schools can offer these services in the general education classroom.

General Education Reform

We are in a unique moment in history to promote the integration mandate of IDEA. My Brother's Keeper, the primary federal initiative to combat the School-to-Prison Pipeline, advocates for the use of strategies developed in special education for youth without disabilities at risk of entering the Pipeline.[104] The initiative hails PBIS, developed and tested for over two decades in special education, as a primary strategy for school-wide discipline reform, and acknowledges that schools can use strategies developed in special education to benefit everyone.

The School-to-Prison Pipeline crisis has highlighted the failure of "one size fits all" education. ED should seize this moment in educational reform to ensure that strategies developed in special education like positive behavioral supports, differentiated education, and supportive services such as mental health counseling benefit all students in the general education classroom. Special educators should take leadership positions in implementing these strategies in general education for all children, with and without disabilities.

Recommendations:

3.19. ED should issue Requests For Proposals (RFPs) and guidance and disseminate information on demonstration projects that utilize universal design for learning and other similar frameworks that ensure all students receive the supports and services they need to succeed in school and divert the School-to-Prison Pipeline.[105]

3.20. ED must take more responsibility for initiating and funding research on the School-to-Prison Pipeline. The research should focus on

[104] My Brother's Keeper Task Force. "My Brother's Keeper Task Force Report to the President."

[105] An example is the OSEP-funded SWIFT Center (School Wide Integrated Framework for Transformation), a national technical assistance center dedicated to implementing a model for educating general and special education students together to improve school-wide academic outcomes. Swift Schools. "Transforming Education." http://www.swiftschools.org/

policies, practices, and procedures that contribute to the School-to-Prison Pipeline and their consequences. The Institute of Education Sciences' National Center for Education Research could lead this important initiative.

Destigmatizing Disability in Diverse Communities

If parents and communities of color view special education as a stigmatizing segregated dumping ground with no educational benefit, it stands to reason that they will continue to avoid special education. Thus the promise of using disability laws to break the School-to-Prison Pipeline hinges on the disability community's and the schools' ability to engage communities of color in meaningful dialogue on the principles and benefits of school inclusion for students with disabilities. The disability rights community has not adequately conveyed the promise of proper IDEA and Section 504 implementation or explained the fundamental disability rights principles of LRE, integration, and inclusion to parents in general, but especially to parents of color and parents of ELLs. Federal agencies should prioritize funding toward helping disability rights organizations foster disability awareness in these communities.

Recommendation:

3.21. Federal agencies should prioritize making funds available for the disability rights community to more fully engage communities of color and take intersectional approaches to School-to-Prison Pipeline reform for students with disabilities.

Child Find

The IDEA "child find" mandate requires each state to ensure that all children with disabilities are "identified, located, and evaluated."[106] Research on the characteristics of students in juvenile detention suggests systemic violations of this requirement. For example, an oft-cited study found that up to 85 percent of children in juvenile detention facilities have disabilities that make them eligible for special education, yet only 37 percent receive services

[106] 20 U.S.C. § 1412(a)(3)(A).

while in school.[107] However, discussing child find violations in the context of the School-to-Prison Pipeline is controversial due to the historical misuse of special education identification, placement, and discipline as a means of excluding poor and students of color. Clearly more research is needed to reconcile anecdotal reports of underrepresentation with the statistical reality of persistent overrepresentation.

OSEP Child Find Monitoring

In practice, failing grades and suspensions can be the results of an unaddressed disability. However, the current IDEA monitoring model does not ensure SEAs and LEAs identify these at-risk students. The only current measures of LEA compliance with child find is Indicator 11, which monitors the timeframe between evaluation and identification, and Indicator 12, which monitors transition between Part C and Part B. As the Court Monitor in *Emma C.* explained, "an LEA can be fully compliant with these indicators yet still have children with disabilities in its jurisdiction who need special education and related services but who have not been identified, located, and evaluated."[108]

OSEP should expand its child find monitoring activities, particularly through the linkage of discipline and school failure with child find. Although IDEA monitoring is behind in this regard, some states have taken a proactive approach. For example, Connecticut law requires the "prompt referral to a Planning and Placement Team of all children who have been suspended repeatedly or whose behavior, attendance, including truant behavior, or progress in school is considered unsatisfactory or at a marginal level of acceptance."[109] Guidance should encourage all states to take similar action to ensure that students with unaddressed needs are referred for RTI, IDEA, or other similar services.[110]

Recommendations:

3.22. ED should increase enforcement of the IDEA child find mandate, including investigating the connection between excessive discipline and child find violations.

---

[107] National Council on Disability, "National Disability Policy: A Progress Report," 2011.
[108] *Emma C. v. Eastin*, 2014 WL 2989946 (N.D. Cal., July 2, 2014).
[109] Regs., Conn. State Agencies §10-76d-7.
[110] See RTI discussion, *supra*.

3.23. OSEP should expand the IDEA child find monitoring system and require SEAs to collect data on the number of students with failing grades or disciplinary records referred for IDEA or RTI services. LEAs should use this data to create systems for referring general education students with failing grades or disciplinary records for IDEA or RTI services.

Teachers Versus Parent Referrals

The source of a special education referral—for example, a parent, teacher, doctor, or social worker—is an overlooked aspect of the disproportionality equation. The collection and study of referral data by source and race would lead to a better understanding of both overrepresentation and underrepresentation because a student is less likely to be "dumped" in special education when it is his or her parent requesting services.

It is well-established that teacher referral is a strong predictor of disproportionality for special education. Some 73 to 90 percent of the students referred by teachers for special education evaluations due to academic problems are found eligible.[111] Less is known about the impact of parent referrals on disproportionality in special education, although anecdotal evidence from special education advocates suggests that schools react much differently to referrals from parents.[112] As explained by Cannon, Gregory, and Waterstone (2013), three clinical professors of law who have experience representing students with disabilities in special education matters, schools often take on a gatekeeping role when parents initiate referrals:

> [W]hen parents express concern about their children's development to school officials or request special education evaluations, school officials sometimes discourage parents from proceeding with the special education process, ignore parental requests altogether, encourage parents to explore interventions outside of school or lower level school-based interventions short of the necessary special education services, or delay far longer than the timelines prescribed by the state in initiating the evaluation process. Not only can these responses dishearten and alienate parents who are often already frustrated, they also cause delays in the evaluation process that need to begin so that students can receive the

---

[111] Harry, Beth, and Janette K. Klingner. *Why are so many minority students in special education?: Understanding race & disability in schools.* Teachers College Press, 2005.

[112] *See, e.g., Ending the School-to-Prison Pipeline: Hearing Before the Subcomm. on the Constitution, Civil Rights, and Human Rights of the S. Comm. on the Judiciary*, 112th Cong. 300-308 (2012) (statement of Arlene B. Mayerson), http://www.gpo.gov/fdsys/pkg/CHRG-112shrg86166/pdf/CHRG-112shrg86166.pdf.

special education services they require to make meaningful academic progress.[113]

There is a dearth of research on special education referrals in general, let alone parent-initiated referrals. Scholars have attributed this to the fact that there are no databases that track referrals, particularly compared to the numerous large, national databases tracking eligibility data.[114] The few studies where scholars have analyzed special education referrals by source were limited to individual school districts.[115] NCD encourages further research and federal monitoring of this important yet overlooked aspect of the disproportionality equation.

Recommendations:

3.24. ED should require SEAs and LEAs to keep data on both the race of students referred for IDEA assessments and the source of these referrals, paying particular attention to parental referrals.

3.25. More research on the source of special education referrals is needed to better understand both overrepresentation and underrepresentation. Researchers should explore the impact of parent referrals on disproportionality in special education and use this data to investigate correlations between race, the source of referral, and ultimate eligibility outcomes.

Transition Planning

Successful transition to higher education, competitive integrated employment, and other value-added postschool activities is another key to breaking the School-to-Prison Pipeline for students with disabilities. In the 2004 reauthorization of IDEA, Congress required that, beginning no later than age 16, a student's IEP must include measurable postsecondary goals related

---

[113] Cannon, Y. Z., Michael Gregory & Julie Waterstone, *A Solution Hiding in Plain Sight: Special Education and Better Outcomes for Students with Social, Emotional, and Behavioral Challenges*, 41 Fordham Urb. L.J. 403, 438-439 (2013).

[114] Hosp, John L., and Daniel J. Reschly. "Referral rates for intervention or assessment a meta-analysis of racial differences." *The Journal of Special Education* 37, no. 2 (2003): 67-80.

[115] Gottlieb, Jay, Barbara W. Gottlieb, and Sharon Trongone. "Parent and teacher referrals for a psychoeducational evaluation." *The Journal of Special Education* 25, no. 2 (1991): 155–167.

to training, education, employment, and, where appropriate, independent living skills.[116] The IEP also must specify the transition services needed to assist the student in reaching those goals.[117] The term "transition services" means a coordinated set of activities for a child with a disability that—

> **(A)** Is designed to be within a results-oriented process, that is focused on improving the academic and functional achievement of the child with a disability to facilitate the child's movement from school to postschool activities, including postsecondary education, vocational education, integrated employment (including supported employment), continuing and adult education, adult services, independent living, or community participation;
> **(B)** Is based on the individual child's needs, taking into account the child's strengths, preferences, and interests; and
> **(C)** Includes instruction, related services, community experiences, the development of employment and other postschool adult living objectives, and, when appropriate, acquisition of daily living skills and functional vocational evaluation.[118]

For this framework to ensure successful transition, SEAs and LEAs must first and foremost maintain high expectations for students with disabilities. Many general and special educators often underestimate the potential of students with disabilities and steer them toward noncompetitive and segregated work placements, such as sheltered workshops. Educators must hold high expectations for all students with disabilities and provide the type of transition services that will assist students in meeting these high expectations.

SEAs and LEAs must also strengthen the nexus between the student's IEP and IEP/transition planning. Although a student's IEP must include transition goals by age 16, the actual transition planning should start much earlier. Middle school is an appropriate starting point, and a student's IEP should have transition goals and services in place by eighth or ninth grade that reflect high expectations and that will continue throughout his or her high school career.

Schools' focus on compliance with required IEP procedures prevents them from identifying the real needs of children and their families and collaboratively developing services to meet those needs. For example, the composition of an IEP team may satisfy the IEP requirements, but is often not the group of people who are most knowledgeable about the child and his or her

[116] 20 U.S.C. § 1414 (d)(1)(A)(i)(VIII).
[117] Ibid.
[118] 20 U.S.C. § 1401(34).

family. This is a problem at all stages of the IEP process, but it particularly impacts transition planning because of the emphasis on the student's strengths, interests, and postschool objectives.

Improved collaboration between the federal agencies that serve students with disabilities during transition would also improve the School-to-Prison Pipeline trajectory. A 2012 report from the U.S. Government Accountability Office (GAO) found that the Departments of Education, Health and Human Services (HHS), and Labor (DOL) and the Social Security Administration (SSA) coordinate transition activities to some degree, but their coordination has limitations and they also do not assess the effectiveness of their efforts. The GAO further found that it is difficult for all students with disabilities and their families to navigate the multiple federal programs that provide transition services, but that students with disabilities in the juvenile justice or criminal justice systems are more likely to face difficulties because they tend not to be aware of or connected to adult service providers.[119]

The GAO urged these agencies to adopt a broader interagency strategic approach to addressing longstanding challenges in providing transition services to students with disabilities:

> Given the multiple agencies involved in supporting this population, in conjunction with multiple eligibility criteria and definitions established in statute, the lack of such a strategy is a missed opportunity to break down coordination barriers and work across agency boundaries. Only then can agencies systemically address persistent transition challenges and improve outcomes for students with disabilities.[120]

NCD supports this call for an interagency approach to improving transition outcomes for at-risk students with disabilities but also calls for greater collaboration between federal agencies and state and local entities such as Centers for Independent Living, Councils on Developmental Disabilities, or state departments of social services and rehabilitation. Many explained that they have clients who are involved in several systems at once (e.g., special education and child welfare), yet there is no coordination between the respective agencies providing services, and at times the agencies actually work at cross-purposes with each other. The federal agencies must prioritize efforts to integrate these agency efforts.

---

[119] Ibid.
[120] Ibid.

Recommendations:

3.26. ED and SEAs must maintain high expectations for students with disabilities and provide the type of transition services that will assist students in meeting these high expectations. They must also require schools to begin transition planning earlier than age 16 to help students better prepare for their chosen postschool objectives.

3.27. LEAs must ensure that IEP team members participating in transition planning are knowledgeable about the child and his or her family, including, for example, school staff who may have a strong relationship with the student but who are not required IEP team members under IDEA.

3.28. ED, HHS, DOL, SSA, and other agencies coordinating transitions services must form an interagency body to brainstorm and adopt a broader interagency strategic approach to addressing longstanding challenges in providing transition services to students with disabilities. The agencies must solicit input from and prioritize improved collaboration with state and local entities as well.

SECTION 4: ADDRESSING RACIAL DISPARITIES IN SPECIAL EDUCATION

NCD believes that robust special education and related services and strict adherence to IDEA procedural protections are critical to breaking the School-to-Prison Pipeline for students with disabilities. Yet persistent racial disparities within the class of students with disabilities caught in the pipeline raise questions of unconscious racial bias that may combine with discrimination on the basis of disability to contribute to the crisis.[121] Efforts to break the pipeline must then also address these unconscious, or implicit, racial biases in a straightforward manner.

[121] Kim, Losen, and Hewitt. *The School-to-Prison Pipeline: Structuring Legal Reform.*

Stereotyping and Implicit Bias

During the Atlanta meeting, Dan Losen, Director of the Center for Civil Rights Remedies at UCLA, provided a practical example of how stereotyping and implicit bias may influence an educator's perception of a student behavior:

> [Implicit bias] affects our perceptions. So here I am a white male teacher; I did teach for 10 years. I see kids in the hallway milling about. If they're a bunch of white kids, I'm a white male, maybe I think they're loitering. I will approach them and say, "Come on, move on to your class." If I'm a white male and these are black or Latino youth, I might think there is gang activity. Maybe I'll call the school resource officer. Maybe that kid has a weapon. I'm not so comfortable. I don't know these kids' parents. I don't feel comfortable calling their parents. . . . I may not be thinking this consciously, but it might affect what I'm actually seeing.

A growing body of research on stereotyping and implicit bias supports this notion that implicit bias influences educators' perceptions and contributes to racial disparities in discipline. A number of studies have shown that administrators dole out harsher punishment to students of color than white students for the same or similar behavior.[122] The potential for these unconscious stereotypes and biases to influence decision making is higher when subjective judgments are involved.[123]

The various special education processes, including child find, assessment, and IEP development, are similarly susceptible to implicit racial biases. With regard to child find, advocates report that school districts often cite the "social maladjustment"[124] or "environmental, cultural, or economic disadvantage"[125] exceptions to IDEA eligibility when refusing initial parent, guardian, or caretaker requests to evaluate students of color. For example, the Disability Rights Education and Defense Fund (DREDF) cited a letter from a Northern California school district to their client, an African American foster child with severe emotional and learning issues that discounted a possible disability

[122] Nicholson-Crotty, Sean, Zachary Birchmeier, and David Valentine. "Exploring the Impact of School Discipline on Racial Disproportion in the Juvenile Justice System." *Social Science Quarterly* 90, no. 4 (2009): 1003–1018; Skiba, Russell J., Robert H. Horner, Choong-Geun Chung, M. Karega Rausch, Seth L. May, and Tary Tobin. "Race is not neutral: A national investigation of African American and Latino disproportionality in school discipline." *School Psychology Review* 40, no. 1 (2011): 85.

[123] Hart, Melissa. "Subjective decisionmaking and unconscious discrimination." *Alabama Law Review* 56 (2005): 741.

[124] 34 C.F.R. § 300.8(c)(4)(ii) (emotional disturbance).

[125] 34 C.F.R. § 300.8(c)(10)(ii) (specific learning disability).

because of the student's "frequent moves," "limited school experience," and "social maladjustment."[126] A child's harsh life circumstances should not be used as the reason to refuse to assess for IDEA eligibility, just as it should not be used as a proxy for disability.

Another area vulnerable to implicit racial biases is assessment. School psychologists often find students of color ineligible for special education because their behavior is believed to be willful or purposeful and not related to a disability.[127,128] Instead, psychologists will diagnose these students with conditions such as oppositional defiant disorder (ODD) and conduct disorder (CD), which are inappropriately classified as non-IDEA eligible conditions.[129] In other instances, schools violate IDEA by refusing to assess students until their families submit medical documentation from a physician.[130] Even when families are able to submit medical proof of learning difficulties such as ADHD, schools still deny IDEA eligibility on the basis that these conditions are "co-morbid" with ODD or CD. The fact that over half of youth in the juvenile justice system have ODD or CD suggests that schools are failing to serve many students with coexistent IDEA-eligible conditions.[131]

Fortunately, research suggests that it is possible to recognize implicit bias in oneself and learn techniques to overcome such perceptions and increase

---

[126] This Prior Written Notice is on file with the authors.

[127] Courts have interpreted the IDEA social maladjustment exception as a distinction between deliberate, purposeful behavior and disability-related behavior. *See Torrance Unified Sch. Dist. v. E.M.*, No. CV 07-2164 (C.D. Cal. Aug. 28, 2008) ("[A] student is socially maladjusted, when the student acts in deliberate noncompliance with known social demands or expectations . . . or when the student's behavior is controlled, predictable, and purposeful"); *E.S. v. Fairfax County Sch. Bd.*, 134 F.3d 659, 664 (4th Cir. 1998), *citing In re Sequoia Union High Sch. Dist.*, 1987-88 ELHR Dec. 559:133, 135 (N.D. Cal. 1987) ("[S]ocially maladjusted [is] a persistent pattern of violating societal norms with lots of truancy, substance . . . abuse, i.e., a perpetual struggle with authority, easily frustrated, impulsive, and manipulative").

[128] Stereotypes of course also contribute to the overrepresentation of students of color in special education. Students of color are more likely to be found eligible under the categories of "emotional disturbance" and "intellectual disability." IDEA Data Center. 2012 IDEA Part B Child Count and Educational Environments.

[129] Merrell, K. W. and Hill M. Walker. "Deconstructing a definition: Social maladjustment versus emotional disturbance and moving the EBD field forward." *Psychology in the Schools* 41 (2004):899.

[130] *N.B. V. Hellgate Elementary Sch. Dist.*, 541 F.3d 1202, 1209 (9th Cir. 2008).

[131] National Collaborative on Workforce and Disability, "Improving Transition Outcomes for Youth Involved in the Juvenile Justice System: Practical Considerations." *Info Brief* 25 (March 2010). http://www.ncwd-youth.info/sites/default/files/Improving_Outcomes_for_Youth_Involved_in_Juvenile_Justice.pdf.

positive social interactions.[132] For example, police training often incorporates these methods.[133] Schools however have been much more resistant to such training due to the current lack of proven, school-based methodologies. At the Atlanta meeting, DREDF Directing Attorney Arlene Mayerson stated that advocates could establish the efficacy of school-based implicit bias interventions by "developing experts in this field to give us more insight into how bias actually operates in school systems."[134] With proven methodologies, school administrators will likely be more open to addressing the impact of implicit bias.

Another barrier is the general difficulty educators, particularly white educators, have in discussing race and racism. In a recent briefing paper for the influential Discipline Disparities: Research-to-Practice Collaborative explained that this reticence to talk frankly about issues of race prevents schools from even considering the steps needed to fix racial discipline disparities:

> Imagine a school district with consistently low reading achievement scores; yet within that district, an unwritten code prevented staff from explicitly discussing the topic of reading. Obviously, the failure to address the central problem would guarantee that reading deficits would persist over time. In the same way, when we don't discuss and then address the racial dynamics of our racially disproportionate discipline, racial disparities in discipline continue to worsen over time.[135]

Addressing this attitudinal barrier is critical. School personnel must understand that addressing implicit biases is not an admission that one is racist. Implicit biases are deep-seated attitudes that operate outside conscious awareness and may even be in direct conflict with a person's stated beliefs and values.[136] As this cutting-edge body of research grows, researchers will need schools to be willing participants in their efforts to reduce racial disparities.

---

[132] Carter, Prudence, Russell Skiba, Mariella Arredondo, and Mica Pollock. "You Can't Fix What You Don't Look At: Acknowledging Race in Addressing Racial Discipline Disparities." *Discipline Disparities: A Research to Practice Collaborative* (December 2014). http://www.indiana.edu/~atlantic/wp-content/uploads/2014/12/Acknowledging-Race_121514.pdf.

[133] Ibid.

[134] Oral statement of Arlene Mayerson during discussion at the Stakeholder Forum to Receive Testimony about the School-to-Prison Pipeline of the National Council on Disability. October 6, 2014. Atlanta, GA.

[135] Carter, Skiba, Arredondo, and Pollock. "You Can't Fix What You Don't Look At: Acknowledging Race in Addressing Racial Discipline Disparities."

[136] Ibid.

Recommendations:

4.1. ED, DOJ, and SEAs should issue RFPs to develop instruments and procedures to evaluate implicit racial and disability bias in schools where minorities are overrepresented in identification, discipline, or segregated settings. It is critical that we understand how implicit bias works in the school environment if we are ever to remedy the overrepresentation of minorities in these areas. For underrepresentation, scholars should examine whether racial bias influences school district gatekeeping, particularly with regard to denials of IDEA eligibility on the basis of "social maladjustment," "environmental, cultural, or economic disadvantage," or "willful or deliberate conduct."

4.2. ED, DOJ, and SEAs should make implicit bias training a core requirement of enforcement agreements and compliance reviews by:

- Including implicit bias training requirements for schools and school districts found to have racial disparities in discipline, juvenile justice referrals, or access to programs and resources;
- Require SEAs receiving federal dollars with schools or school districts that have high levels of disproportionality to provide quarterly training and professional development on implicit bias;
- Issue guidance or develop training materials on the relationship between school discipline and exposure to harassment, violence, and trauma (i.e., criminalization of victims' response to this exposure); and
- In grant making, target funds and give priority to districts that do cultural competence and implicit bias training, do training on the impact of trauma on student behavior, and that have mental health services integrated into school settings (e.g., universal screenings).

4.3. Schools should voluntarily implement implicit bias and stereotyping training to enhance staff awareness of their implicit or unconscious biases.

Race-Conscious Positive Behavioral Interventions and Supports

Separate from the individualized positive behavioral interventions and supports available under IDEA is School-wide Positive Behavioral

Interventions and Supports (SWPBIS), a systemic and data-driven approach to improving school discipline environments. SWPBIS emphasizes changing the underlying attitudes and policies concerning how student behavior is addressed.[137] Advocates have had success implementing SWPBIS systems pursuant to IDEA, ADA, and Section 504 administrative complaints.[138] ED similarly supports this framework and offers grants and technical assistance to help schools with its implementation.[139]

ED should continue to support SWPBIS for students with disabilities but must encourage schools implementing this framework to do so in a racially and culturally competent manner. SWPBIS has been successful in reducing office disciplinary referrals, decreasing rates of school suspension, and improving school climate. But research shows that without specific attention to issues of race and culture, implementation has not always successfully reduced racial/ethnic disparities in office referrals and suspension.[140] For example, very few districts that currently receive IDEA funding to implement SWPBIS disaggregate their data by race and ethnicity. Schools implementing SWPBIS or other similar frameworks such as RTI must pay specific attention to race and ethnicity data.[141]

Recommendation:

4.4. OSEP must require grantees implementing SWPBIS to disaggregate data by race and ethnicity to ensure that reductions in total disciplinary actions coincide with reductions in racial and ethnic disparities.

---

[137] Losen, D., D. Hewitt, and I. Toldson. "Eliminating excessive and unfair exclusionary discipline in schools: Policy recommendations for reducing disparities." (2014).

[138] Southern Poverty Law Center. "Palm Beach County Schools Reach Agreement with SPLC, Advocates to Reduce Exclusionary School Discipline."

[139] Office of Special Education Programs. *Positive Behavioral Interventions and Supports.* www.pbis.org.

[140] Carter, Skiba, Arredondo, and Pollock. "You Can't Fix What You Don't Look At: Acknowledging Race in Addressing Racial Discipline Disparities."

[141] Losen, Hewitt, and Toldson. "Eliminating Excessive and Unfair Exclusionary Discipline in Schools."

SECTION 5: DATA COLLECTION ENFORCEMENT AND EXPANSION

The availability of accurate, disaggregated data is invaluable for advocates and policymakers working to break the School-to-Prison Pipeline for students with disabilities. Although access to data has increased over the last decade, public entities often fail to enforce and comply with existing data collection and reporting requirements. Moreover, there are a number of areas where Congress and relevant administrative agencies should expand current data collection systems to include certain groups of students, such as students with disabilities who have Section 504 plans, who are largely unaccounted for.

Enforcement and Compliance Issues

Many statutes and regulations affecting students with disabilities contain strong data disaggregation, collection, and reporting requirements. However, noncompliance with these provisions is common and enforcement lacking. To facilitate the identification of problems and areas to target solutions, the Federal Government, SEAs, LEAs, and individual schools must fulfill their respective data collection and reporting duties.

Civil Rights Data Collection

The Civil Rights Data Collection (CRDC) is a mandatory data collection conducted by ED.[142] The CRDC's purpose is to obtain data related to the nation's public schools[143] and school districts' obligation to provide equal educational opportunity. To fulfill this goal, the CRDC collects a variety of information disaggregated by race/ethnicity, sex, limited English proficiency, and disability.

Although CRDC data reporting is mandatory, many public schools and school districts grossly underreport data relating to students with disabilities.

[142] The CRDC is authorized under the statutes and regulations implementing Title VI of the Civil Rights Act of 1964, Title IX of the Education Amendments of 1972, Section 504 of the Rehabilitation Act of 1973, and under the Department of Education Organization Act (20 U.S.C. § 3413). The regulations implementing these provisions can be found at 34 CFR § 100.6(b); 34 CFR § 106.71; and 34 CFR § 104.61.

[143] In the CRDC, "public schools" refers to traditional public schools (preschool through 12th grade), alternative schools, career and technical education schools, and charter schools. U.S. Department of Education, Office for Civil Rights. "About the Civil Rights Data Collection." http://ocrdata.ed.gov/downloads/AboutTheCRDC.pdf.

This is particularly evident in several categories relevant to the School-to-Prison Pipeline, including retention, bullying and harassment, suspensions and expulsions, incidents of restraints and seclusion, and school-based arrests. The lack of access to this data prevents both advocates and the schools themselves from identifying problems and instituting much needed interventions. Districts and schools currently face no ramifications from the Department for underreporting.

Recommendations:

5.1. ED should take affirmative steps to enforce the mandatory CRDC data reporting requirements.

5.2. Public schools (including charter schools) and LEAs must fully comply with the mandatory CRDC data reporting requirements, including the requirements to submit data on suspensions, expulsions, incidents of restraints and seclusion, and school-based arrests disaggregated by disability.

IDEA Discipline Data Collection and Reporting Requirements

Among the comprehensive data collection and reporting provisions in Section 618 of IDEA is the directive for SEAs to provide the Department with data on the "incidence and duration of disciplinary actions by race, ethnicity, limited English proficiency status, gender, and disability category, of children with disabilities, including suspensions of 1 day or more."[144] As explained below, many SEAs neither report nor examine this data in a manner consistent with IDEA requirements.

Public Reporting

IDEA requires SEAs to report disaggregated discipline data to the public.[145] According to a July 2014 survey conducted by the Center for Civil Rights Remedies, SEA noncompliance with this mandate is widespread. There are only 16 SEAs that publicly report discipline data, and only eight of these disaggregate at least some of the data by race and ethnicity.[146] Only one state—New Mexico—is in full compliance.[147]

---

[144] 20 U.S.C. § 1418(a)(1)(D).

[145] 20 U.S.C. § 1418(a).

[146] Center for Civil Rights Remedies. "Nation-wide Survey of State Education Agencies' Online School Disciplinary Data for Students with Disabilities," (2014). http://civilrightsproject.ucla.edu/resources/projects/center-for-civil-rights-remedies/school-to-prison-folder/online-

Recommendation:

5.3. ED should ensure full compliance with the IDEA provision requiring SEAs to publicly report discipline data disaggregated by race and ethnicity.

State Examination of Suspension and Expulsion Rates

IDEA requires SEAs to examine disaggregated discipline data each fiscal year to determine if discrepancies are occurring in the rate of long-term suspensions and expulsions of students with disabilities (i) among LEAs in the state; or (ii) compared to such rates for students without disabilities within such agencies.[148] If such discrepancies are occurring, the SEA must require the affected LEAs to revise their policies, procedures, and practices relating to the development and implementation of IEPs, the use of positive behavioral interventions and supports, and procedural safeguards, to ensure that such policies, procedures, and practices comply with IDEA.[149]

Such annual examinations, to the extent SEAs actually perform them, are rarely reported to the public. Lawyers, community advocates, legislators, and other interested stakeholders must wait for the biennial CRDC survey results to compare the discipline rates of students with disabilities to students without disabilities. Moreover, the CRDC numbers do not present stakeholders with an up-to-date picture of a district. For example, ED-OCR released the 2011–2012 statistics in March 2014.

Recommendation:

5.4. ED must ensure SEAs comply with the IDEA requirement to examine discipline data disaggregated by race and ethnicity each fiscal year to determine if significant discrepancies are occurring in the rate of long-term suspensions and expulsions of students with disabilities among (i) among local educational agencies in the state; or (ii) compared to such rates for students without disabilities within such agencies. ED should report the results of these examinations to the public.

data-resources/nation-wide-survey-of-state-education-agencies2019-online-school-disciplinary-data.

[147] Ibid.

[148] 20 U.S.C. § 1412(a)(22).

[149] Ibid.

5.5. SEAs must comply with the aforementioned IDEA provision requiring examination of long-term suspension and expulsion rates and report the results of these examinations to the public.

Restraint and Seclusion

Statistics show students with disabilities are disproportionately restrained and secluded in school. Currently, students served by IDEA represent 12 percent of the student population but 58 percent of those placed in seclusion and 75 percent of those physically restrained.[150] Like discipline, seclusion and restraint implicates the provision of FAPE. Accurate data on incidents of restraint and seclusion would shed light on this epidemic and force schools to reform their practices. As mentioned earlier, the CRDC survey only collects data on restraint and seclusion every other year.[151] OSEP should issue guidance which explains that using seclusion and restraints instead of positive behavioral interventions may form the basis of a finding of noncompliance with FAPE. Furthermore, OSEP should clearly indicate that schools cannot use seclusion and restraint as punishment, and if they are, they must report such incidents as a disciplinary action.[152]

There is also a clear need for Congressional action on the issue of restraint and seclusion. There is no federal law, regulation, or binding guidance[153] governing restraint and seclusion, and enforcement at the state level involves a patchwork of laws, regulations, nonbinding guidelines, and even utter silence (Butler 2014).[154] Moreover, in a February 2014 report, the Senate Health, Education, Labor, and Pensions Majority Committee found that under current

---

[150] Civil Rights Data Collection. Data Snapshot: School Discipline.

[151] U.S. Department of Education, Office for Civil Rights. "About the Civil Rights Data Collection."

[152] In a 2007 policy memorandum, OSEP clarified that the definition of "disciplinary incident" encompasses much more than formal suspension or expulsion: "The type of disciplinary action refers to, at a minimum, data on both in-school and out-of-school suspensions and expulsions, but could also include other disciplinary actions (e.g., exclusion from extracurricular activities)." Office of Special Education Programs. "Policy Memorandum 07-09." April 2007. https://www2.ed.gov/policy/speced/guid/idea/letters/2007-2/osep0709 disproportionality2q2007.doc.

[153] In "Restraint and Seclusion: A Resource Document," the U.S. Department of Education states that the document "does not set forth any new requirements, does not create or confer any rights for or on any person or require specific actions by any state, locality, or school district." U.S. Department of Education, Restraint and Seclusion: Resource Document, Washington, D.C., 2012. https://www2.ed.gov/policy/seclusion/restraints-and-seclusion-resources.pdf.

[154] Butler, Jessica. "How Safe Is The Schoolhouse? An Analysis of State Seclusion and Restraint Laws and Policies." Autism National Committee (2014). http://www.autcom.org/pdf/HowSafeSchoolhouse.pdf.

law, "a family whose child has been injured, experienced trauma, or, in the worst case, has died as a result of the use of seclusion or restraints practices in a school has little or no recourse through school procedures or the courts."[155] A 2009 GAO report analyzed cases of alleged abuse, including 20 deaths, related to the use of restraint, and stated that it "could not find a single Web site, federal agency, or other entity that collects information on the use of these methods or the extent of their alleged abuse."[156]

Recommendations:

5.6. OSEP should issue policy guidance on the improper use of seclusion and restraints and the implications for a finding of non-compliance for failing to provide FAPE.

5.7. Congress should take appropriate action to address the need for a uniform approach to restraint and seclusion and ensure the safety and dignity of every student. Restraint and seclusion legislation should, at a minimum: (1) limit the use of restraint and seclusion to cases where there is imminent danger of physical injury to the student or others at school; (2) provide criteria and steps for the proper use of restraint or seclusion; (3) promote the use of positive reinforcement and other, less restrictive behavioral interventions; and (4) require states to establish reporting and data collection standards.

Results Driven Accountability

NCD and the broader disability rights community support OSEP's recent shift to results driven accountability (RDA) and its increased focus on test scores and other outcomes for students with disabilities. However, OSEP omitted many important indicators in the new Part B Results Matrix. The most glaring omissions are: Indicator 1 (percent of youth with IEPs graduating from high school with a regular diploma compared to all youth), Indicators 4A and 4B (significant discrepancies, by race and ethnicity, in the rates of suspensions and expulsions), and Indicator 5 (LRE; in fact, the RDA does not have any LRE accountability measures). Graduation, discipline, and inclusion rates are

---

[155] U.S. Senate Health, Education, Labor, and Pensions Committee. "Dangerous Use of Seclusion and Restraints in Schools Remains Widespread and Difficult to Remedy: A Review of Ten Cases," (2014). http://www.help.senate.gov/imo/media/doc/Seclusion%20and%20Restraints%20Final%20Report.pdf.

[156] U.S. Government Accountability Office, "Seclusions and Restraints: Selected Cases of Death and Abuse at Public and Private Schools and Treatment Centers" (2009). http://www.gao.gov/new.items/d09719t.pdf.

just as important as test scores in determining successful outcomes for students with disabilities and should be included in the Part B Results Matrix.

Moreover, the OSEP Part B Compliance Matrix only monitors SEA disciplinary practices through Indicator 4B, which measures significant discrepancies, by race and ethnicity, in the rates of suspensions and expulsions greater than 10 days. By limiting compliance monitoring to suspensions and expulsions greater than 10 days, OSEP fails to hold SEAs accountable for racial and ethnic disparities in total disciplinary removals.

Recommendations:

5.8. OSEP should amend its Part B Results Matrix to include Indicator 1 (graduation rates), Indicators 4A and 4B (suspension and expulsion rates), and Indicator 5 (LRE). Moreover, OSEP should create a new compliance indicator that holds SEAs responsible for reporting all discipline disparities, not just disparities in suspensions and expulsions greater than 10 days.

Legislative and Administrative Data Collection Recommendations

The upcoming reauthorizations of IDEA, Juvenile Justice Delinquency Prevention Act (JJDPA), and the Elementary and Secondary Education Act (ESEA) present opportunities for Congress to reinforce and expand existing data collection and reporting frameworks affecting students with disabilities at risk of entering the School-to-Prison Pipeline.

Amendments to IDEA Section 618

As mentioned earlier, Section 618 of IDEA includes comprehensive data collection and reporting requirements.[157] But to facilitate more nuanced, intersectional analyses of disciplinary data, Congress should amend the Section to require additional data collection and reporting requirements that facilitate analyses of how race, gender, ELL status, economic status, grade level, and type of offense affect discipline patterns beyond simple suspension and expulsion counts. An amendment to the disciplinary data provisions in Section 618 would also be a logical way for OSEP to collect and report

[157] 20 U.S.C. § 1418.

disaggregated data on informal school removals, including shortened school days and "sent homes."

Recommendation:

5.9. OSEP should continue to require SEAs to collect and report discipline data from every school district in the country pursuant to Section 618. The school discipline data should include:

- The number of suspensions, including unduplicated counts (similar to the CRDC), the total number of suspensions, and the duration of suspensions;
- The reasons for each suspension, as incident data on less serious and more subjective offenses is critical in understanding the effect of school discipline policies;
- Data broken down by grade (elementary, middle, and high schools);
- Reporting of cross-sectional data (i.e., reporting data publicly to look at the confluence of two or more groups);
- Discipline disaggregated by poverty;
- Data on first-time offender by the punishment he or she received; and
- An effective method to collect and report disaggregated data on informal school removals, including shortened school days and "sent homes."

IDEA Part C Infant and Toddler Discipline Data

The CRDC collected data on preschool suspensions for the first time in its 2011–2012 survey. When released in March 2014, the data revealed shocking disparities in the suspension rates of black and male preschoolers. African American children make up 18 percent of preschool enrollment, but 48 percent of preschool children were suspended more than once.[158] African American boys received more than three out of four out-of-school preschool suspensions.[159]

The CRDC survey, however, showed that preschools are not disproportionately suspending students with disabilities. Students receiving IDEA services represent 22 percent of preschool enrollment, but 19 percent of the students suspended once and 17 percent of the students suspended more

[158] Civil Rights Data Collection. Data Snapshot: Early Childhood Education. March 21, 2014. http://www2.ed.gov/about/offices/list/ocr/docs/crdc-early-learning-snapshot.pdf.

[159] Ibid.

than once.[160] It is unclear whether there are racial or ethnic disparities within these numbers because the available disability data is not disaggregated. Furthermore, it is possible that many of the suspended preschool students of color had unidentified disabilities.

The 2011–2012 CRDC preschool suspension data is likely just the tip of the iceberg. Part C of IDEA, which covers early intervention services for infants and toddlers with disabilities, does not require SEAs to collect discipline data for this population, disaggregated or otherwise. Requiring Part C entities to report disaggregated discipline data would ensure yearly access to data, increase child find compliance, and prevent the needless suspension of young children with disabilities.

Recommendation:

5.10. ED should require SEAs to compile disaggregated data on the discipline of infants and toddlers with disabilities receiving services under IDEA Part C.

Access to Juvenile Justice Statistics

SEAs must include students with disabilities in correctional facilities when collecting and reporting data pursuant to IDEA.[161] This data is limited because not all students with disabilities receive IDEA services. Some have Section 504 plans while others may have unidentified disabilities. But outside of IDEA, access to data on youth with disabilities in the juvenile justice and criminal justice systems is limited. For example, the statistics compiled by the Office of Juvenile Justice and Delinquency Prevention pursuant to the JJDPA do not account for disability status.[162] Going forward, all major reauthorizations and regulatory undertakings that affect youth in the juvenile justice and criminal justice systems must include provisions requiring the collection of data disaggregated by race, ethnicity, ELL, and disability status.

Recommendations:

5.11. All upcoming major reauthorizations and regulatory undertakings that affect youth in the juvenile justice and criminal justice

---

[160] Ibid.

[161] 34 C.F.R. § 300.2(b).

[162] Office of Juvenile Justice and Delinquency Prevention (OJJDP). "Easy Access to Juvenile Populations, 1990–2013." http://www.ojjdp.gov/ojstatbb/ezapop/.

systems (e.g., IDEA, ESEA, and JJDPA) must include provisions requiring the collection of data disaggregated by race, ethnicity, gender, ELL, and disability status. The data should address important questions such as:

- What are the characteristics of individuals entering the juvenile justice system?
- What is the quality of the education these individuals receive in juvenile detention facilities?
- What are the characteristics of individuals exiting the juvenile justice system?
- In what educational environments are students placed upon reentry?

Section 504 of the Rehabilitation Act

Section 504 requires LEAs to provide accommodations to students with disabilities who qualify for services under Section 504 but are otherwise not eligible for IDEA services. While OCR is responsible for the civil rights enforcement of Section 504 with state and local educational agencies,[163] the Department leaves implementation and compliance to the state level. Consequently, there is no federal or state oversight, monitoring, or accountability for the services provided to students with disabilities that have a 504 plan; nor the educational, and ultimately, the transition outcomes achieved by these students.

Recommendation:

5.12. OCR should develop a Section 504 enforcement, monitoring, and technical assistance system to hold SEAs and LEAs accountable for the delivery of effective services to students with disabilities who have Section 504 plans.

SECTION 6: OTHER FEDERAL LAWS IMPACTING STUDENTS WITH DISABILITIES

This report primarily focuses on the potential of IDEA, Section 504, ADA, and other disability laws to break the School-to-Prison Pipeline. There

[163] 34 C.F.R. Part 104.

are however other significant federal laws that overlap to impact students with disabilities at risk of entering the pipeline, including the McKinney-Vento Homeless Education Assistance Act ("McKinney-Vento Act"), ESEA, JJDPA, and Title VI of the Civil Rights Act of 1964. This section discusses these laws and sets forth relevant policy and advocacy recommendations.

McKinney-Vento Homeless Education Assistance Act

The McKinney-Vento Act is a federal law that ensures immediate enrollment and educational stability for homeless children and youth.[164] The Act requires schools to enroll and serve homeless children and youth consistent with their "best interest," even if the students lack normally required documents such as immunization records or proof of residence. It also ensures that homeless children and youth have transportation to and from their school of origin.

The educational stability piece of McKinney-Vento is critical to breaking the School-to-Prison Pipeline. Homeless families that lack residency documentation can assert McKinney-Vento protections to prevent discriminatory attempts to oust their children. Too many homeless families however are unaware of these protections. School districts must better educate families on their rights under this law and appoint knowledgeable McKinney-Vento coordinators who can work with families in an effective and sensitive manner. Schools must also cease the targeting of students with disabilities in fraudulent enrollment investigations. These activities could arguably amount to discrimination under Section 504 or Title II of the ADA. More research and advocacy is needed in this area to better understand the nature of these potentially discriminatory activities.

Recommendation:

6.1. SEAs and LEAs must improve implementation of the McKinney-Vento Homeless Education Assistance Act to ensure homeless students have a stable education environment and avoid truancy. LEAs in particular must better educate families on their rights under the law and appoint knowledgeable McKinney-Vento coordinators who can work with families in an effective and sensitive manner.

---

[164] 42 U.S.C. § 11431 *et seq.*

Elementary and Secondary Education Act

Congress last reauthorized the ESEA in 2002 when it passed the No Child Left Behind Act. Reauthorization of the ESEA is long overdue but is likely to come sometime in 2015. In February 2015, members of the NDRN Civil Rights Roundtable met to create legislative recommendations for the ESEA reauthorization that specifically address disproportionality in discipline and juvenile justice referrals. NCD supports the group's final recommendations and incorporates them into this document.[165]

Recommendation:

6.2. Congress should adopt the School-to-Prison Pipeline recommendations drafted by the members of the NDRN Civil Rights Roundtable.

Juvenile Justice and Delinquency Prevention Act

The JJDPA[166] is the central federal law relating to youth in contact with the juvenile justice system. The Act supports delinquency prevention efforts and offers financial incentives for states to promote youth safety at the "front end" of the juvenile justice system by: (1) protecting incarcerated youth from contact with adult offenders; (2) reducing unnecessary incarceration by diverting youth who engage in low-level misbehavior (e.g., status offenses); and (3) addressing the disproportionate number of youth of color who come into contact with the juvenile justice system.

Congress last amended the JJDPA in 2002 and the Act is long overdue for reauthorization. NCD has identified the following key legislative and administrative recommendations for the next reauthorization: (1) eliminate the valid court order (VCO) exception; (2) improve coordination between the status offense system and the special education system; (3) create increased funding to juvenile justice advocates, including creating a Juvenile Justice Protection & Advocacy Program.

---

[165] *See* ESEA policy recommendations from the NDRN Civil Rights Roundtable task force. http://www.ndrn.org/images/Documents/Issues/Education/Hearing_Testimony_STPP_121212_FINAL_edb_thoughts.pdf.

[166] Pub. L. No. 93-415 (1974).

Valid Court Order Exception

The JJDPA prohibits the incarceration of young people who engage in status offense behaviors, meaning conduct that would not be a crime if committed by an adult. Examples of status offenses include truancy, curfew violations, incorrigibility, running away, and underage possession and/or consumption of alcohol or tobacco.[167]

In the 1980s, Congress added the VCO exception, which allowed judges to detain youth who commit status offenses in secure/locked facilities if they find the youth to be in contempt or in violation of a VCO.[168] This change has had a devastating effect on the nation's youth. In 2012 alone, it was used to incarcerate children more than 7,000 times nationwide.[169] Research shows that locking up status offenders leads to worse outcomes for children and their communities.[170]

On December 11, 2014, Senators Sheldon Whitehouse (D-RI) and Chuck Grassley (R-IA) introduced S.B. 2999, a bill that requires states to phase out their usage of the VCO exception over three years. Going forward, the elimination of the VCO must remain a nonnegotiable aspect of the JJDPA reauthorization.[171]

Recommendation:

6.3. Congress must amend the JJDPA to prohibit the use of the VCO exception to securely confine youth adjudicated for status offenses and enable relevant federal agencies to provide research, training, and technical assistance to assist state and local status offense system reform efforts.

---

[167] National Disability Rights Network. "Including a Juvenile Justice Protection & Advocacy Program in the JJDPA Reauthorization Act." http://www.ndrn.org/issues/juvenile-justice/327-juvenile-frequently-asked-questions-.html.

[168] Coalition for Juvenile Justice (2014). "Making the Case for Status Offense Systems Change: A Toolkit." Washington, DC: Coalition for Juvenile Justice. http://www.juvjustice.org/sites/default/files/resource-files/Judicial%20Leadership%20Toolkit%20Web.pdf.

[169] Coalition for Juvenile Justice. *Juvenile Justice* Monitor: December 2014/January 2015. http://campaign.r20.constantcontact.com/render?ca=49892347-ac92-4fb2-8a95-cdacae0e5acf&c=3021a2f0-7e49-11e3-a163-d4ae529a8639&ch=30dd2ac0-7e49-11e3-a1a3-d4ae529a8639.

[170] Coalition for Juvenile Justice (2014). "Making the Case for Status Offense Systems Change: A Toolkit."

[171] Coalition for Juvenile Justice. *Juvenile Justice* Monitor: December 2014/January 2015.

Status Offenses Reform for Youth with Disabilities

JJDPA-funded reform activities must specifically target students with disabilities. Young people too often enter the status offense system because of unidentified or unaddressed disabilities. Improved coordination between the status offense and special education systems would ensure that IDEA, Section 504, and ADA violations are uncovered during the adjudication of status offense charges. Neither schools nor juvenile courts consistently follow existing safeguards designed to facilitate coordination between them. For example, a rarely enforced IDEA provision requires schools reporting a crime committed by a child with a disability to ensure that copies of the student's special education and disciplinary records are sent to the appropriate authorities for their consideration.[172]

An effective way to improve coordination between these two systems is to train juvenile defense attorneys, probation officers, juvenile court judges, and prosecutors in special education and civil rights law. With improved understanding of their clients' special education rights, these attorneys could identify child find or FAPE violations and pursue special education services to divert status offense system involvement.[173] For example, after implementing an intensive, special education law training program for court-appointed delinquency and child welfare attorneys, Washington, D.C., became the only jurisdiction in the country in which a substantial percentage of low-income parents had access to counsel willing and able to provide special education representation.[174] The availability of counsel to these families enabled them to prevail in the majority of due process complaints filed, an experience that stands in contrast to that in most other jurisdictions where success with the filing of due process complaints is much less prevalent.[175]

---

[172] 20 U.S.C. §1415(k)(6)(B)

[173] Tulman, Joseph B. 2010. "Using Special Education Advocacy to Avoid or Resolve Status Offense Charges." In Representing Juvenile Status Offenders. Edited by Sally Small Inada & Claire S. Chiamulera. Washington, DC: American Bar Association. http://www.americanbar.org/content/dam/aba/migrated/child/PublicDocuments/rjso_chapter6.authcheckdam.pdf.

[174] Tulman, Joseph B., et al., *Reversing the School-to Prison Pipeline: Initial Findings from the District of Columbia on the Efficacy of Training and Mobilizing Court-Appointed Lawyers to Use Special Education Advocacy on Behalf of At-Risk Youth*, 18 U.D.C. L.Rev ___ (2015) (forthcoming).

[175] *Id.*

Recommendations:

6.4. OSEP and SEAs must enforce, and LEAs must comply, with 20 U.S.C. Sec. 1415(k)(6)(B), a provision that requires schools reporting a crime committed by a child with a disability to ensure that copies of the student's special education and disciplinary records are sent to the appropriate authorities for their consideration.

6.5. Congress should amend the JJDPA to include funding for status offense reform that targets students with disabilities and encourages coordination between the status offense and special education systems.

6.6. Congress should create and support programs that train probation officers, juvenile court judges, prosecutors, court-appointed attorneys representing youth, and public defenders on special education and civil rights laws. Improved understanding of these laws could help divert at-risk from the juvenile justice system and ensure they receive necessary education services.

Creation and Funding of JJDPA Juvenile Advocacy Programs

Due to economic and other related issues, there is a dearth of advocates and attorneys available to assist youth with juvenile justice and discipline issues. Congress and administrative agencies should create and support programs that increase the number of attorneys available to represent youth at risk of entering the School-to-Prison Pipeline. For example, ED could increase funding to Parent Training and Information Centers (PTIs) and Community Parent Resource Centers (CPRCs) and encourage them to create juvenile justice-focused projects. Bar associations could also implement mandatory pro bono hour rules and offer continuing legal education (CLE) credits in exchange for taking juvenile justice cases. Increased use of law school clinics is yet another way to increase at-risk youth's access to attorneys.

NDRN has set forth a viable proposal for the creation of a federal Juvenile Justice Protection and Advocacy (JJ P&A) program in the reauthorized JJDPA.[176] The need for a JJ P&A is clear. An overwhelming number of youth with special education needs come into contact with the juvenile justice system, clogging the courts and overcrowding juvenile justice facilities at great expense to state and local governments. Adding a JJ P&A program to the JJDPA would increase oversight and accountability for compliance with the

---

[176] National Disability Rights Network. "Including a Juvenile Justice Protection & Advocacy Program in the JJDPA Reauthorization Act."

Act and promote public safety by identifying youth with disabilities and the services they need to reduce delinquent conduct, recidivism, and future contact with the juvenile justice system.

Creating a JJ P&A program taps into an existing nationwide Protection & Advocacy (P&A) system[177] for individuals with disabilities—a well-established, federally mandated network in every state that has a proven track record of success for 40 years. P&A agencies have the expertise, experience, and infrastructure to increase their advocacy in the juvenile justice system immediately but have been unable to expand because of a lack of resources.[178]

Recommendations:

6.7. ED should increase funding to PTIs and CRPCs and encourage them to target services toward youth at risk of entering the School-to-Prison Pipeline.

6.8. State and local bar associations should implement mandatory pro bono hour rules and offer CLE credits in exchange for taking juvenile justice cases.

6.9. Congress should create a Juvenile Justice Protection & Advocacy program in the JJDPA Reauthorization Act of 2015 (S. 1699). The system would tap into the disability expertise of the P&A network to improve the ability of the overburdened juvenile justice system to effectively meet the needs of youth with disabilities.

Title VI of the Civil Rights Act of 1964

There are ample opportunities for administrative agencies and advocates to use Title VI of the Civil Rights Act of 1964 in conjunction with special

---

177 Since 1975, P&As have been mandated by various federal statutes to provide legal representation and other advocacy services to adults and children with any type of disability—including but not limited to those with intellectual, emotional, sensory, and physical disabilities. There is a P&A agency in every state, the District of Columbia, and five U.S. territories. Additionally, there is a Native American P&A in the Four Corners region of the United States. Each year, the P&A system serves approximately 100,000 individuals with disabilities through individual case representation and systemic advocacy. P&As pursue legal, administrative, and other appropriate remedies under all relevant federal, state, and local laws, such as the Americans with Disabilities Act (ADA), the Individuals with Disabilities Education Act (IDEA), and Section 504 of the Rehabilitation.

178 National Disability Rights Network. "Including a Juvenile Justice Protection & Advocacy Program in the JJDPA Reauthorization Act."

education laws to improve outcomes for students of color with disabilities. ED, DOJ, and other relevant agencies must coordinate their enforcement efforts and specifically target the disproportionate discipline and juvenile justice referrals of students of color with disabilities. Moreover, ED-OCR and DOJ should target Title VI complaints toward addressing special education disparities and resource inequity.

Coordination of Federal Title VI and IDEA Enforcement

For Title VI to improve outcomes for students of color with disabilities, the various administrative agencies enforcing the law must coordinate enforcement of Title VI and IDEA/Section 504/ADA and target enforcement efforts on the specific issue of disproportionality in school removals and juvenile justice referrals.

Recommendations:

6.10. Representatives from OSEP, ED-OCR, and DOJ's Civil Rights Division, among others, should meet to coordinate enforcement of Title VI and IDEA/Section 504/ADA and bolster enforcement efforts on the specific issue of disproportionality in school discipline and juvenile justice referrals. One goal of the meetings should be to ensure that all agencies are utilizing the full range of enforcement options, including but not limited to:

- Directed funding;
- Partial withholding;
- Compliance agreements; and
- Referrals for litigation.

6.11. ED should make referrals to DOJ for litigation enforcing these laws. Litigation could be an alternative to withholding of funds, which can be difficult to effectuate and counterproductive in some circumstances.

6.12. ED and DOJ should enforce Title VI regulations for every entity receiving federal financial assistance, especially those that do not receive the funds directly. Enforcement must apply to both disparate treatment (whether intentional or not) and disparate impact.

6.13. ED and DOJ should expand the scope of Title VI investigations to include:

- The extent to which school discipline policies disproportionately impact girls of color and conduct litigation to remedy school disciplinary practices that specifically involve the intersection of race and gender discrimination or stereotypes (i.e., improved coordination between Title VI and Title IX of the Education Amendments of 1972 enforcement activities); and

- Either encourage or support the efforts of U.S. Attorneys who investigate possible civil rights violations by public, charter, and private schools.

Title VI and Special Education Resource Equity

One potential way for advocates to address the racial disparities in special education is through Title VI resource inequality complaints. On October 1, 2014, ED-OCR issued a policy letter to public schools on their legal obligation under Title VI to provide students with equal access to resources without regard to race, color, or national origin.[179] Although the letter did not directly address disability, OCR made it clear it would analyze the quality of IDEA services during its Title VI investigations:

> Equal educational opportunity requires that all students, regardless of race, color, or national origin, have comparable access to the diverse range of courses, programs, and extracurricular activities offered in our Nation's schools. . . . Therefore, OCR assesses the types, quantity, and quality of programs available to students across a school district to determine whether students of all races have equal access to comparable programs both among schools and among students within the same school. . . . OCR may consider the overall quality and adequacy of special education programs at the school level, including identification, evaluation, and placement procedures as well as the quality and appropriateness of services and supports provided to students with disabilities to determine whether schools serving more students of color have comparable supports and services in place for students with disabilities.[180]

OCR also stated that it would consider staff-to-student ratios and the training, certification, and years of experience of special education support staff such as paraprofessionals, school psychologists, specialized therapy providers (e.g., speech, physical, and occupational therapists), and social workers to determine whether these critical personnel are supporting students with disabilities on a nondiscriminatory basis.[181] OCR also vowed to

[179] U.S. Department of Education, Office for Civil Rights. "Dear Colleague Letter," October 1, 2014. http://www2.ed.gov/about/offices/list/ocr/letters/colleague-resourcecomp-201410.pdf.
[180] Ibid.
[181] Ibid.

investigate the quality of both physical buildings and educational technologies to ensure they are accessible to students with disabilities.[182]

The OCR resource inequality policy letter presents a number of creative and strategic opportunities for advocates. For example, advocates could combine resource inequality and discriminatory school discipline allegations in one OCR complaint. Discipline cases can be stigmatizing and uncomfortable for students and their families. Advocates could ease these fears by connecting disciplinary actions with a lack of adequate resources. Title VI allegations could also of course be combined with Section 504 and ADA Title II allegations. Advocates must explore these ideas and other types of creative approaches to more effectively address race and disability issues together.

Recommendation:

6.14. Advocates should use Title VI administrative complaints to address racial disparities in special education. Examples include strategically combining racial inequality and discriminatory discipline allegations into one complaint.

SECTION 7: PARTICIPANT LIST

NCD Stakeholder Forum to Receive Testimony about the School-to-Prison Pipeline
Monday, October 6, 2014
Shepherd Center, 2020 Peachtree St, Atlanta, GA 30309

Meeting Participants:
Alice Abrokwa, Skadden Fellow
Judge Bazelon Center for Mental Health Law
Washington, DC

Gary Blumenthal, Council Member
National Council on Disability
Sudbury, MA
Robert Borrelle, Equal Justice Works Fellow

[182] Ibid.

Disability Rights Education & Defense Fund
Berkeley, CA

Courtney Bowie, Senior Staff Attorney
American Civil Liberties Union – Racial Justice Program
New York, NY

Ira Burnim, Legal Director
Judge Bazelon Center for Mental Health Law
Washington, DC

Lawrence Carter, Public Affairs Specialist
National Council on Disability
Washington, DC

Thomas Chapman, MPH, ED
The HSC Foundation
Washington, DC

Isaiah Chase II, College Student
Atlanta, GA

Rebecca Cokley, Executive Director
National Council on Disability
Washington, DC

Jonathan Feldman, Attorney
Empire Justice Center
Rochester, NY

Chester A. Finn, Council Member
National Council on Disability
Albany, NY

Janel George, Education Policy Counsel
NAACP Legal Defense and Educational Fund
Washington, DC

Susan Henderson, Executive Director
Disability Rights Education & Defense Fund
Berkeley, CA

Debra Jennings, Co-Director
Statewide Parent Advocacy Network/
Center for Parent Information & Resources (CPIR)
Newark, NJ

Talina Jones, Chair
NY Early Intervention Coordinating Council
Syracuse, NY

Narell Joyner, Consultant
Charlotte, NC

Jerri Katzerman
Southern Poverty Law Center
Montgomery, AL

Bill Lann Lee, Partner
Lewis Feinberg Lee Renaker & Jackson
Oakland, CA

Janice Lehrer-Stein, Council Member
National Council on Disability
San Francisco, CA

Talila Lewis
Helping Educate to Advance the Rights of the Deaf (HEARD)
Rochester, NY

Daniel Losen, Director
Center for Civil Rights Remedies at UCLA's Civil Rights Project
Boston, MA

Kamilah Oni Martin-Proctor, Council Member
National Council on Disability
Washington, DC

Arlene Mayerson, Directing Attorney
Disability Rights Education & Defense Fund
Berkeley, CA

Robin Miller, Education Advocate
Disability Rights Education & Defense Fund
Berkeley, CA

Ari Ne'eman, Council Member
National Council on Disability
Silver Spring, MD

Benro T. Ogunyipe, Council Member
National Council on Disability
Chicago, IL

Curtis Richards, Director
Center for Workforce Development
Washington, DC

Jeff Rosen, Chairperson
National Council on Disability
Rockville, MD

Lynnae Ruttledge, Council Member
National Council on Disability
Vancouver, WA

Thomas Saenz, President and General Counsel
MALDEF
Los Angeles, CA

Katherine D. Seelman, Co-Vice Chair
National Council on Disability
Pittsburgh, PA

Brenda Shum, Director, Educational Opportunities
Lawyers' Committee for Civil Rights
New York, NY

Diane Smith Howard, Senior Staff Attorney
National Disability Rights Network
Washington, DC

Clyde Terry, Council Member
National Council on Disability
Concord, NH

Cheryl Theis, Education Advocate
Disability Rights Education & Defense Fund
Berkeley, CA

Royal P. Walker, Jr., Co-Vice Chair
National Council on Disability
Jackson, MS

Michael Yudin, Acting Assistant Secretary
Office of Special Education and Rehabilitative Services
Washington, DC

SECTION 8: LIST OF ACRONYMS

ADA	Americans with Disabilities Act
ADHD	Attention Deficit/Hyperactivity Disorder
ALJ	Administrative Law Judge
BIP	Behavioral Intervention Plan
CD	Conduct Disorder
CDE	California Department of Education
CLE	Continuing Legal Education
CPRC	Community Parent Resource Center
CRDC	Civil Rights Data Collection
DOJ	U.S. Department of Justice
DOL	U.S. Department of Labor
DREDF	Disability Rights Education and Defense Fund
ED	U.S. Department of Education
ELL	English Language Learner
ESEA	Elementary and Secondary Education Act
FAPE	Free and Appropriate Public Education

FBA	Functional Behavioral Assessment
GAO	U.S. Government Accountability Office
HHS	U.S. Department of Health and Human Services
ID	Intellectual Disability
IDEA	Individuals with Disabilities Education Act
IEP	Individualized Education Plan
JJ P&A	Juvenile Justice Protection and Advocacy Program
JJDPA	Juvenile Justice Delinquency Prevention Act
LEA	Local Education Agency
LRE	Least Restrictive Environment
NAEP	National Assessment of Educational Progress
NCD	National Council on Disability
NDRN	National Disability Rights Network
OCR	U.S. Department of Education Office for Civil Rights
ODD	Oppositional Defiant Disorder
OSEP	Office of Special Education programs
OSERS	Office of Special Education and Rehabilitative Services
P&A	Protection and Advocacy
PTI	Parent Training and Information Center
RDA	Results Driven Accountability
RTI	Response to Intervention
SEA	State Education Agency
SLD	Specific Learning Disability
SSA	Social Security Administration
SWPBIS	School-wide Positive Behavioral Interventions and Supports
VCO	Valid Court Order

In: Students with Disabilities in the Justice System ISBN: 978-1-63483-749-1
Editor: Amelia Guerrero

Chapter 2

DEAR COLLEAGUE LETTER ON THE INDIVIDUALS WITH DISABILITIES EDUCATION ACT FOR STUDENTS WITH DISABILITIES IN CORRECTIONAL FACILITIES[*]

Melody Musgrove and Michael K. Yudin

Dear Colleague:

We are writing to focus your attention on the educational needs of students with disabilities who are in correctional facilities[1] and the requirements of Part B of the Individuals with Disabilities Education Act (IDEA or IDEA, Part B) as they apply to States, State educational agencies (SEAs), and public agencies (including local educational agencies (LEAs), and responsible noneducational public agencies[2]) in educating these students. Absent a specific exception, all IDEA protections apply to students with disabilities in correctional facilities and their parents.[3] Supporting effective and accountable education for incarcerated and at-risk youth can result in cost savings to the public and enable troubled youth to obtain an education and enhance their future employment

---

[*] This is an edited, reformatted and augmented version of Dear Colleague letter issued by the U.S. Department of Education, Office of Special Education and Rehabilitative Services, December 5, 2014.

options and life choices. As the U.S. Departments of Education (Department) and Justice recently stated, the fact that a student has been charged with or convicted of a crime does not diminish his or her substantive rights or the procedural safeguards and remedies provided under the IDEA to students with disabilities and their parents.[4] This letter also provides information regarding technical assistance and other relevant resources to enhance students' reintegration into the school setting or participation in programs.

Students with disabilities represent a large portion of students in correctional facilities, and it appears that not all students with disabilities are receiving the special education and related services to which they are entitled. National reports document that approximately one third of students in juvenile correctional facilities were receiving special education services, ranging from 9 percent to 78 percent across jurisdictions.[5] States reported that in 2012–2013, of the 5,823,844 students with disabilities, ages 6 through 21, served under IDEA, Part B, 16,157 received special education and related services in correctional facilities.[6] Evidence suggests that proper identification of students with disabilities and the quality of education services offered to students in these settings is often inadequate.[7] Challenges such as overcrowding, frequent transfers in and out of facilities, lack of qualified teachers,[8] inability to address gaps in students' education, and lack of collaboration with the LEA contribute to the problem.[9] Providing the students with disabilities in these facilities the free appropriate public education (FAPE) to which they are entitled under the IDEA should facilitate their successful reentry into the school, community, and home, and enable them to ultimately lead successful adult lives.

This letter is organized into three main areas. The first summarizes the key points in the letter. The second addresses States' and SEAs' responsibilities to students with disabilities in correctional facilities. The third addresses the responsibilities of public agencies, including LEAs, and correctional facilities that operate as LEAs, and noneducational public agencies that are responsible for providing education to students with disabilities in correctional facilities to carry out IDEA requirements. Because the responsibilities of these entities in certain areas overlap, some matters are discussed more than once.

The following are the key points made in this letter regarding IDEA, Part B requirements, as they pertain to students with disabilities:

- Absent a specific exception, all IDEA protections apply to students with disabilities in correctional facilities and their parents.

Shared Responsibility to Provide FAPE

- Every agency at any level of government that is involved in the provision of special education and related services to students in correctional facilities must ensure the provision of FAPE, even if other agencies share that responsibility.
- States must have interagency agreements or other methods for ensuring interagency coordination in place so that it is clear which agency or agencies are responsible for providing or paying for services necessary to ensure FAPE for students with disabilities in correctional facilities.

SEA Responsibility and Personnel Qualifications

- SEAs must exercise general supervision over all educational programs for students with disabilities in correctional facilities (unless covered by an exception) to ensure that their educational programs meet State education standards and IDEA, Part B requirements. This responsibility includes monitoring public agencies that are responsible for providing FAPE to students with disabilities in correctional facilities.
- SEAs must make annual determinations on the performance of correctional facilities in their State if those facilities operate as their own LEAs.
- SEAs must ensure that students with disabilities, including those in correctional facilities, are appropriately included in general State and districtwide assessments, including assessments conducted under section 1111 of the Elementary and Secondary Education Act of 1965, as amended (ESEA), to the extent that the ESEA requires that those students be included in those assessments.
- The State Advisory Panel must include representatives from the State juvenile and adult corrections agencies, and include other agencies involved in the financing or delivery of services to students with disabilities.
- States and their public agencies must establish and maintain qualifications to ensure that personnel providing special education and related services, including those serving students with disabilities in correctional facilities, are appropriately and adequately prepared and

trained. Public school special education teachers in correctional facilities must be "highly qualified," as defined by IDEA and its implementing regulations, and related services personnel and paraprofessionals in correctional facilities must meet State qualifications for those personnel, as described in IDEA and its implementing regulations. SEAs must monitor to ensure that there are appropriate special education teachers in schools and education programs within correctional facilities.

Child Find and Evaluation

- States and their public agencies must have child find policies and procedures in place to identify, locate, and evaluate students who are in correctional facilities who may have a disability under the IDEA and are in need of special education and related services, regardless of the severity of their disability and consistent with the State's child find and eligibility standards. This responsibility includes students who have never been identified as a student with a disability prior to their entry into the facility.
- Students suspected of having a disability who need special education and related services must be evaluated, subject to applicable parental consent requirements, in a timely manner, even if the student will not be in the facility long enough to complete the evaluation. If a student transfers from an LEA to a correctional facility in the same school year after the evaluation has begun, and the responsibility for FAPE transfers as well, both agencies must coordinate assessments to ensure that a timely evaluation occurs.

FAPE in Least Restrictive Environment

- When a student with an individualized education program (IEP) transfers to a correctional facility in the same State in the same school year, the new public agency (in consultation with the parents) must provide the student with FAPE through services that are comparable to those described in the student's IEP from the previous public agency until the new public agency either adopts the previous agency's IEP, or develops and implements a new IEP for the student.
- Unless there is a specific exception, all IEP content requirements apply to students with disabilities in correctional facilities, including,

but not limited to, a statement of: (1) the student's present levels of academic achievement and functional performance; (2) measurable annual academic and functional goals; and (3) the special education and related services and supplementary aids and services that will be provided to the student to enable him or her to advance appropriately toward attaining his or her IEP goals and to be involved in and make progress in the general education curriculum—that is, the same curriculum as for nondisabled students.

- To ensure that students with disabilities in correctional facilities continue to receive FAPE, public agencies must have policies and procedures to ensure that the relevant records of students with disabilities who move to, and from, correctional facilities are transferred as expeditiously as possible," and also must take reasonable steps to appropriately transmit those records to facilitate the student's transition to or from the correctional facility.
- The IDEA requirements related to least restrictive environment (LRE) apply to the education of students with disabilities in correctional facilities. IEP teams or placement teams must make individualized placement decisions, and may not routinely place all students with disabilities in correctional facilities in classes that include only students with disabilities, even if this means creating placement options or using other arrangements, to the maximum extent appropriate to the student's needs. This may include, for example, having special education and general education teachers co-teach in the regular classroom.
- Public agencies must comply with all applicable IDEA secondary transition requirements to facilitate eligible students' movement from secondary education in the correctional facility to appropriate post-school activities.

Due Process and Discipline

- The IDEA due process protections apply to students in correctional facilities and their parents, including requirements related to providing any required written notices in language understandable to the general public and in the native language of the parent or other mode of communication used by the parent, unless it is clearly not feasible to do so.

- Any exclusion from the classroom is particularly harmful for students with disabilities in correctional facilities. In general, even in the presence of disciplinary concerns, because correctional facilities are run by public entities, their obligation to ensure that special education and related services are provided to eligible students with disabilities continues.
- A student with a disability in a correctional facility who violates a code of student conduct is entitled to the protections in the IDEA discipline procedures that must be afforded to all students with disabilities. These protections apply regardless of whether a student who violates a code of student conduct is subject to discipline in the facility or removed to restricted settings, such as confinement to the student's cell or "lockdown" units. In any event, a removal from the current educational placement that results in a denial of educational services for more than 10 consecutive school days, or a series of removals that constitute a pattern that total more than 10 school days in a school year is a change in placement, which, in turn, requires a manifestation determination under the IDEA.

STATES' AND STATE EDUCATIONAL AGENCIES' RESPONSIBILITIES

Responsibility for Ensuring FAPE in Correctional Facilities

Every agency at any level of government that is involved in the provision of special education and related services to students with disabilities in correctional settings must ensure the provision of FAPE, even if other agencies share that responsibility (34 CFR §300.2(b)(1)(iv)).[10]

Regardless of the structure in a State, the State, as the IDEA, Part B grantee, has ultimate responsibility for ensuring FAPE is made available to all eligible students with disabilities residing in State and local juvenile and adult correctional facilities. This responsibility applies to correctional facilities with which the State contracts to provide education, including special education and related services (34 CFR §§300.2(b)(1)(iv), 300.101, and 300.149(a)). Indeed, the requirements in IDEA, Part B apply to all political subdivisions of a State[11] that provide special education and related services to students with disabilities, including State and local juvenile and adult correctional facilities, regardless of whether that agency receives funds under Part B (34 CFR §300.2(b)(1)(iv) and (2)).

States have different administrative structures or arrangements for providing education, including special education and related services, to students with disabilities in correctional facilities. These arrangements include assigning the responsibility for providing special education and related services in correctional facilities to: (1) the SEA; (2) the correctional facility as an LEA; (3) the LEA where the correctional facility is located or another LEA; (4) a noneducational public agency[12] through an interagency agreement or other mechanism for interagency coordination that meets the requirements in 34 CFR §300.154; and (5) a transfer of authority pursuant to 34 CFR §300.149(d).[13]

When the State assigns responsibility for providing FAPE to a noneducational public agency, the IDEA expressly requires the Chief Executive Officer of a State, or his or her designee, to ensure that an interagency agreement or other mechanism for interagency coordination is in effect between each noneducational public agency and the SEA (34 CFR §300.154(a)). The purpose of this requirement is to ensure that the responsibility for the provision of FAPE for all students with disabilities is clear and that services necessary to ensure FAPE are provided in a timely and appropriate manner. This is particularly important in the context of correctional facilities, where it is not uncommon for multiple agencies to share responsibility for the operation of distinct functions within the same facility. The State may meet this requirement through a contract, or other methods, such as a State statute or regulation, or a signed interagency agreement, between respective agency officials that clearly identifies the responsibilities of each agency[14] (34 CFR §300.154(b) and (c)(1) and (2)).

Interagency agreements, or other mechanisms for interagency coordination, must include provisions relating to: (1) the financial responsibility of each agency for providing special education and related services,[15] including reimbursement terms;[16] (2) the resolution of interagency disputes; and (3) the coordination and delivery of special education and related services (34 CFR §300.154(a)). In addition to these required provisions, as a best practice, States are encouraged to include additional provisions in their interagency agreements or other mechanisms to ensure that the needs of students with disabilities will be properly identified and appropriately addressed so that these students timely receive the special education and related services to which they are entitled under the IDEA. For example, States should consider including provisions that identify the: (1) location of IEP

Team meetings and, if not within the correctional facility, the responsibility for ensuring that the student is transported to the meeting, if appropriate for the student to attend[17]; and (2) where applicable, the responsibility of the correctional facility to ensure that it grants appropriate access to facilities to all personnel necessary to implement the IDEA requirements. Granting appropriate access may be essential to ensure that evaluations (including the administration of any necessary assessments or other evaluation materials), IEP Team meetings, and the provision of required special education and related services occur in a timely manner.

Accountability, Data Collection, and Reporting

SEAs must ensure that all students with disabilities, including those in correctional facilities, are appropriately included in all general State and districtwide assessment programs, including assessments described in section 1111 of the ESEA, to the extent that the ESEA requires that students in correctional facilities be included in those assessments.[18] Students with disabilities who are required to take any general State assessment during the time that they are confined to a correctional facility must be provided appropriate accommodations on the State assessment, or administered an appropriate alternate assessment, if determined to be necessary for the student by the student's IEP Team (34 CFR §§300.160(a) and 300.320(a)(6)). The SEA must also exercise general supervision over all educational programs for students with disabilities in correctional facilities (34 CFR §300.149) to ensure that such programs meet the education standards of the SEA and IDEA requirements. As part of this responsibility, the SEA must monitor public agencies that are responsible for providing FAPE in correctional facilities (34 CFR §300.149)).[19] Furthermore, SEAs must make annual determinations about the performance of each correctional facility that is its own LEA (34 CFR §300.600(a)(2)). States must include students with disabilities in correctional facilities when collecting and reporting data, including data reported in connection with IDEA section 618 data submissions and in the State's Annual Performance Report.

Personnel Qualifications

The IDEA personnel qualifications requirements continue to apply even though personnel are providing special education and related services to students with disabilities in a correctional facility. Accordingly, the SEA must: (1) establish and maintain qualifications to ensure that those personnel necessary to carry out the purposes of the IDEA are appropriately and adequately prepared and trained, including that those personnel have the content knowledge and skills to serve students with disabilities (34 CFR §300.156(a)); (2) ensure that qualifications of related services personnel and paraprofessionals are consistent with any State-approved or State-recognized certification, licensing, registration, or other comparable requirements that apply to the professional discipline in which those personnel are providing special education or related services (34 CFR §300.156(b)); and (3) ensure that each person employed as a public school special education teacher in the State is "highly qualified" (34 CFR §§300.18 and 300.156(c)).

Child Find

The SEA must have child find policies and procedures in effect that ensure that all age-eligible students with disabilities, including those in correctional facilities, who are in need of special education and related services, are identified, located, and evaluated, regardless of the severity of their disability (34 CFR §300.111(a)(1)(i)).[20] To meet these requirements, we strongly encourage SEAs to develop child find policies and procedures that address the unique challenges associated with identifying students with disabilities in correctional facilities. For example, State child find policies and procedures frequently focus on teachers and staff in traditional schools, as well as the local medical community. State child find policies and procedures should also include those individuals in the community who come in contact with students in the juvenile justice system, including intake staff, social workers, probation officers, truant officers, police, and medical and mental health professionals who treat students in correctional facilities, as well as other staff in the juvenile justice system and in correctional facilities.

Surrogate Parents

In circumstances where the appointment of a surrogate parent is necessary, as described in 34 CFR §300.519(a), the SEA must make reasonable efforts to ensure the assignment of a qualified surrogate parent not more than 30 days after a public agency determines that the student needs a surrogate parent. The surrogate parent may represent the student in all matters relating to the identification, evaluation, and educational placement of the student, and the provision of FAPE. The surrogate parent must meet the knowledge, skills, impartiality, and other required criteria described in the IDEA and its implementing regulations. 34 CFR §300.519(d), (g), and (h).

Transfer of Parental Rights at Age of Majority

The IDEA permits, but does not require, a State to transfer all rights accorded to parents under the IDEA to students who are in an adult or juvenile, State or local correctional facility when the student with a disability reaches the age of majority under State law, unless the student has been determined to be incompetent under State law (34 CFR §300.520). Once a student reaches the age of majority, questions regarding guardianship as an adult may arise. As a best practice, it is advisable for students, families, and the IEP Team to consider alternatives to guardianship first, in order to preserve a young person's legal independence to the maximum extent possible.

State Advisory Panel

To implement the supports and interventions needed by students with disabilities entering, attending classes, and exiting the corrections system, requires significant collaboration and communication across agencies. The State Advisory Panel (SAP) is in a position to advise on such matters, particularly since it must include representatives from the State juvenile and adult corrections agencies, and other agencies involved in the financing or delivery of services to students with disabilities (34 CFR §300.168). As an advisory body, the SAP can work to address concerns regarding interagency record sharing, coordinated efforts between agencies, shared databases, and other related activities.[21]

RESPONSIBILITIES OF PUBLIC AGENCIES, INCLUDING LEAS, CORRECTIONAL FACILITIES, AND NONEDUCATIONAL PUBLIC AGENCIES, TO ENSURE A FREE APPROPRIATE PUBLIC EDUCATION

As noted above, in *Responsibility for Ensuring FAPE in Correctional Facilities*, States have different methods for assigning responsibility for FAPE for students with disabilities in correctional facilities. In some cases, the correctional facility is itself an LEA or is a noneducational public agency with the responsibility for FAPE. For the purposes of this letter, we refer to public agency or LEA interchangeably when discussing specific responsibilities. However, these requirements apply to any public agency, LEA, correctional facility, and noneducational public agency responsible for providing FAPE to children with disabilities in correctional facilities.

FAPE and Transfer of Records

The rules governing the responsibility for FAPE in connection to students with IEPs who transfer from one public agency to another apply when a student with a disability is in a correctional facility and the responsibility for the provision of FAPE transfers from one public agency (generally an LEA) to another public agency (generally another LEA that is, or includes, the correctional facility).[22] All agencies involved must have policies and procedures that ensure that the education records of students with disabilities who move to, and from, correctional facilities are transferred as expeditiously as possible.

The failure of a public agency to obtain educational records promptly can interfere with the student's ability to receive FAPE and to receive credits towards graduation. Therefore, it is critical that public agencies and correctional facilities have systems in place to ensure compliance with the transmittal of records requirements in 34 CFR §300.323(g). Public agencies are encouraged to assign specific staff the responsibility to work with correctional staff to promptly transfer education records to facilitate the student's timely connection to educational or training activities.

The new public agency in which the student enrolls must take reasonable steps to promptly obtain the student's records (including the IEP and supporting documents and any other records relating to the provision of special education or related services to the student) from the previous public agency in which the student was enrolled, pursuant to the Family Educational Rights and Privacy Act (FERPA)[23] (34 CFR §300.323(g)). The previous public agency in which the student was enrolled must take reasonable steps to promptly respond to the request from the new public agency (34 CFR §300.323(g)(2)).[24] In addition, the parent of a student with a disability may provide a copy of the IEP directly to the new public agency.

However, if, after taking reasonable steps, the new public agency is not able to obtain the IEP from the parent or from the previous public agency, the new public agency must, at a minimum, place the student in the regular school program, conduct an evaluation, and make an eligibility determination pursuant to 34 CFR §§300.304 through 300.306, if the new public agency determines an evaluation is necessary (34 CFR §300.323(f)(1)). Although the new public agency is not required to provide special education and related services to the student because it would be unable to determine what constitutes comparable services for the student without an IEP from the previous public agency, excluding the student from all educational services is not permissible. Moreover, even if the new public agency is unable to obtain the student's IEP from the previous public agency, if the new public agency decides that an evaluation is necessary because it has reason to suspect that the student has a disability, nothing in the IDEA or its implementing regulations would prevent the agency from providing special education services to the student while the evaluation is pending, subject to an agreement between the parent and the agency.[25]

Child Find and Evaluations

LEAs are responsible for implementing the SEA's child find policies. It is not sufficient to assume that a student that enters a correctional facility is not a student with a disability simply because he or she has not yet been identified as such. Therefore, LEAs should work with individuals who are most likely to come into contact with students in the juvenile justice system (see *Child Find* above) to identify students suspected of having a disability and ensure that a timely referral for an evaluation is made. To determine if a student has a disability, a parent or a public agency may initiate a request for an evaluation. Moreover, the evaluation of a student suspected of having a disability must occur once parental consent has been obtained even if the student will not be in the facility long enough to complete the process.

Generally, the IDEA requires completion of initial evaluations within 60 days of receiving parental consent for the evaluation or within the State-established time frame (34 CFR §300.301(c)(1) (procedures for initial evaluation) and 34 CFR §300.9 (definition of consent)). In addition, it is important to note that assessments and other evaluation materials used to assess a student must be selected and administered so as not to be discriminatory on a racial or cultural basis and must be provided and administered in the student's native language or other mode of communication and in the form most likely to yield accurate information, unless it is clearly not feasible to so provide or administer (34 CFR §300.304(c)(1)(i) and (ii)).

If the student is transferred to a correctional facility in the same school year, in the same State or in a different State, after the previous LEA has begun but has not completed the evaluation, both public agencies must ensure that assessments are coordinated to ensure completion of the evaluation. This must occur as necessary and as expeditiously as possible (34 CFR §300.304(c)(5)). However, the relevant time frame does not apply when the following two conditions are present: (1) the new school district is making sufficient progress to ensure prompt completion of the evaluation; and (2) the parent and new school district agree to a specific time when the evaluation will be completed (34 CFR §300.301(d)(2) and (e)). As noted in *FAPE and Transfer of Records* above, 34 CFR §300.323(g) requires public agencies to take reasonable steps to promptly exchange relevant records when a child transfers to a new public agency and enrolls in a new school in the same school year, subject to FERPA. Relevant records could include existing evaluation data on the child, consistent with 34 CFR §300.305. Prompt exchange of any relevant records avoids duplicating previously conducted evaluations, and provides critical data to the new public agency to ensure the timely completion of the evaluation.[26]

Personnel Qualifications and Training

The public agency must ensure that all personnel necessary to fulfill the requirements of the IDEA are appropriately and adequately prepared, subject to the requirements of 34 CFR §300.156, relating to personnel qualifications (34 CFR §300.207).[27] Public agencies should consider including noneducational correctional staff in professional development activities regarding the IDEA, including positive behavioral interventions and supports and discipline procedures, and provide opportunities for discussions across agency staff regarding any problems students with disabilities may experience in correctional facilities.

Individualized Education Programs

All of the IEP content requirements apply to students with disabilities in correctional facilities (34 CFR §300.320),[28] including, but not limited to, a statement of: (1) the student's present levels of academic achievement and functional performance (IEP Teams need to have the student's academic and other school records in order to determine the student's present levels of achievement and performance); (2) measurable annual academic and functional goals; and (3) the special education and related services and supplementary aids and services that will be provided to the student to enable him or her to advance appropriately toward attaining his or her IEP goals and to be involved in and make progress in the general education curriculum (the general education curriculum is the same curriculum provided to students without disabilities in the State).

When a student with an existing IEP from another public agency arrives in a correctional facility in the same State, the facility either must implement the existing IEP or hold an IEP Team meeting to modify the contents of the IEP (34 CFR §300.323(e)). If a student with an existing IEP from another public agency arrives in a correctional facility in a different State, the new public agency either must conduct its own evaluation and make a new eligibility determination pursuant to 34 CFR §§300.304-300.306, if determined to be necessary by the new public agency, or develop and implement a new IEP for the student (34 CFR §300.323(f)). However, as an initial matter, the new public agency, in consultation with the parents, must provide the student FAPE (including services comparable to those described in the student's IEP from the prior public agency) in accordance with 34 CFR §300.323(e) or (f), as appropriate.

When developing or modifying an IEP for a student in a correctional facility, IEP Teams should consider whether there has been an interruption in the provision of special education and related services during the student's transfer to the correctional facility, and how the break in services has affected the type or amount of special education and related services needed to provide FAPE to the student. In addition, the special factors that the IEP Team must consider in developing, reviewing, and revising the IEP of each student with a disability are particularly relevant to students with disabilities in correctional facilities. Among these special factors is the requirement for the IEP Team to consider the use of positive behavioral interventions and supports and other strategies to address behavior in the case of a student whose behavior impedes his or her learning or the learning of others (34 CFR §300.324(b)(2)). Appropriate implementation of these positive behavioral interventions and supports and other strategies to address behavior should ensure that the student is able to benefit from his or her educational program in the correctional facility, and hasten the student's transition from the facility and reentry into the community.

Students identified with a disability either before or during incarceration in a correctional facility, who: (1) did not transfer to the correctional facility with an IEP; or (2) were not attending or enrolled in school at the time of incarceration, must have a meeting to develop an IEP within 30 days of the determination that the student needs special education and related services (34 CFR §300.323(c)(1)).[29] As soon as possible following the development of the IEP, the public agency must make available special education and related services to the student (34 CFR §300.323(c)(2)). IEP Teams should pay particular attention to those related services that are likely to be required for students in correctional facilities -- for example, counseling, parent counseling and training, psychological services, transportation, and social work services in schools (34 CFR §300.34(c)(2), (c)(8), (c)(10), (c)(14), and (c)(16)).

Least Restrictive Environment

The IDEA emphasizes the importance of educating students with disabilities in regular classes and in extracurricular and other nonacademic activities with nondisabled students to the maximum extent appropriate (34 CFR §§300.114, 300.117, and 300.320(a)(4) and (5)). Therefore, each public agency must ensure that special classes, separate schooling, or other removal of students with disabilities from the regular education environment occurs only when the nature or severity of the disability is such that education in regular classes with the use of supplementary aids and services cannot be achieved satisfactorily (34 CFR §300.114(a)(2)). If a determination is made that a student with a disability cannot be educated satisfactorily in the regular educational environment, even with the provision of appropriate supplementary aids and services, that student then could be placed in a setting other than the regular educational setting. Placement decisions must be made on an individual basis by a group of persons, including the parents, and other persons knowledgeable about the child, the meaning of the evaluation data, and the placement options (34 CFR §300.116(a)). In addition, the IEP must also include an explanation of the extent, if any, to which the student will not participate with nondisabled students in the regular classroom or in extracurricular or other nonacademic activities (34 CFR §300.320(a)(5)).

Each public agency must ensure that a continuum of alternative placements is available to meet the needs of students with disabilities for special education and related services (34 CFR §300.115). These options must be available to the extent necessary to implement the student's IEP. Any alternative placement selected for the student outside of the regular education environment (education with nondisabled peers) must maximize opportunities for the student to interact with nondisabled peers, to the extent appropriate to the needs of the student. Accordingly, IEP Teams must make individualized placement decisions, and may not routinely place all students with disabilities in correctional facilities in classes that include only students with disabilities, even if this means creating a placement that is appropriate for the student, through methods such as having special education and general education teachers co-teach in the regular classroom (34 CFR §§300.116(a) and (b)).

Secondary Transition

There are inherent difficulties associated with reentry from a correctional facility to home or another community environment. Therefore, it is particularly important that public agencies comply with the IDEA requirements related to secondary transition (34 CFR §300.320(b)).[30]

Accordingly, beginning no later than the first IEP to be in effect when the student turns 16 (or younger if determined appropriate by the IEP Team), and updated annually thereafter, the IEP must include: (1) appropriate measurable postsecondary goals based upon age appropriate transition assessments related to training, education, employment, and, where appropriate, independent living skills; and (2) the transition services (including courses of study) needed to assist the student in reaching those goals. In addition, the public agency must invite the student with a disability to attend the student's IEP Team meeting if a purpose of the meeting will be the consideration of the postsecondary goals for the student and the transition services needed to assist the student in reaching those goals, as required in 34 CFR §300.321(b).[31] If the student does not attend the IEP Team meeting, the public agency must take other steps to ensure that the student's preferences and interests are considered.

Moreover, to the extent appropriate, with the consent of the parents or a student who has reached the age of majority, the public agency must invite a representative of any participating agency that is likely to be responsible for providing or paying for transition services (34 CFR §300.321(b)(1)–(3)). Finally, beginning not later than one year before the student reaches the age of majority under State law, the IEP must document that the student has been informed of the student's rights under the IDEA, if any, that will transfer to the student on reaching the age of majority under 34 CFR §300.520 (34 CFR §300.320(c)).

Due Process Protections

All of the due process protections under the IDEA extend to eligible students with disabilities in correctional facilities and their parents. Parents remain required members of the IEP and placement teams and retain all rights under IDEA, Part B unless a court has limited their rights or parental rights have transferred to the student at the age of majority. A parent who disagrees with the public agency on matters arising under the IDEA, including matters arising prior to the filing of a due process complaint, must have the opportunity to resolve the dispute through the mediation process described in 34 CFR §300.506 (34 CFR §300.500). In addition, a parent has the right to file a due process complaint to request a due process hearing on any matter relating to the identification, evaluation, or educational placement of the student, or the provision of FAPE to the student, in accordance with procedures in 34 CFR §§300.507 through 300.518 (34 CFR §300.507(a)(1)). If a student has been assigned a surrogate parent, the due process rights that are available to parents are afforded to the surrogate parent, and the prior written notice and procedural safeguards notice must be provided to the surrogate parent (34 CFR 300.519(g)). Similarly, the surrogate parent may utilize mediation or exercise due process rights on behalf of the student or themselves. (See *Parental Engagement* below for a discussion of affording parents prior written notices in the native language of the parent or other mode of communication used by the parent, unless it is clearly not feasible to do so.)

Discipline Procedures

Any exclusion from the classroom is particularly harmful for students with disabilities in correctional facilities because they often have already lost instructional time due to their involvement in the juvenile justice system. Collaboration between the correctional facility and the public agency responsible for FAPE, if different, is essential to minimize behavioral incidents and avoid disciplinary exclusions from school. For students whose behavior impedes the student's learning, or that of others, the IEP Team must consider, behavioral intervention strategies, including the use of positive behavioral interventions and supports, when developing the initial IEP, or modifying an existing IEP, so as to reduce the need for discipline of students with disabilities (34 CFR §300.324(a)(2)(i)). Public agencies cannot avoid their IDEA obligations, including the discipline procedures, by contracting, transferring them to, or sharing them with another agency.[32] Therefore, we expect that correctional facilities will not use discipline methods that deprive eligible students with disabilities of FAPE.

A student with a disability in a correctional facility who violates a code of student conduct is entitled to the protections that must be afforded to all students with disabilities related to discipline procedures, including those related to a change of placement, manifestation determination, and provision of services beginning with the 11th cumulative day of removal in a school year (34 CFR §§300.530 through 300.536).[33] These disciplinary protections apply regardless of whether a student is subject to discipline in the facility or removed to restricted settings, such as confinement to the student's cell or living quarters or "lockdown" units. In any event, a removal that results in a denial of educational services for more than 10 consecutive school days, or a series of removals that constitute a pattern that total more than 10 school days in a school year, is a change in placement, which, in turn, requires a manifestation determination in accordance with 34 CFR §300.530(e).[34]

Each time a student with a disability in a correctional facility is removed from his or her current educational placement for more than 10 consecutive school days, or each time that the public agency determines that a series of removals constitutes a change of placement, the public agency must: (1) provide services to the student as provided for in 34 CFR §300.530(d) to enable the student to continue to participate in the general education curriculum, although in another setting and to progress toward meeting the goals in the student's IEP; and (2) conduct, as appropriate, a functional behavioral assessment and provide behavioral intervention services and modifications, that are designed to address the behavioral violation so that it does not recur (34 CFR §300.530(d)(1)(ii) and (f)(1)). In addition, within 10 school days of any decision to change the placement of a student with a disability because of a violation of a code of student conduct, the LEA, parent, and relevant members of the student's IEP Team must conduct a manifestation determination (34 CFR §300.530(e)). Specifically, an IEP Team is required to hold a manifestation determination to determine whether the student's conduct in question was caused by, or had a direct and substantial relationship to, the student's disability, or if the conduct in question was the direct result of the failure to implement the IEP. It is particularly important for IEP Teams to review carefully whether the student has, in fact, received the special education and related services that are provided in the student's IEP when making this determination, as the failure to implement an IEP may be more common in some correctional facilities than in traditional schools.

Parental Engagement

Parental[35] engagement in a student's education is particularly important when a student with a disability is in a correctional facility. Parents who remain involved with their child's education while the student is in a correctional facility will be better equipped to provide needed support to the student when he or she exits the facility and returns to the community and/or school. Unless the State has opted to transfer parental rights at the age of majority under 34 CFR §300.520(a) (see *Transfer of Parental Rights at Age of Majority,* above), parents do not lose their rights under the IDEA when their child is placed in a correctional facility, even if the student has been convicted as an adult and incarcerated in an adult prison.

Parents of students in correctional facilities are entitled to receive all "prior written notice" and procedural safeguards notice documents, as required by 34 CFR §§300.503, 300.504, and 300.520(a)(1)(i). The LEA or other responsible public agency must provide the parents with a prior written notice, in accordance with 34 CFR §300.503, a reasonable time before the public agency proposes or refuses to initiate or change the identification, evaluation, or educational placement of a child with a disability, or the provision of FAPE to the child. These notices must be written in language understandable to the general public and provided in the native language of the parent or other mode of communication used by the parent, unless it is clearly not feasible to do so (34 CFR §300.503(c)(1)).[36]

Furthermore, correctional facilities may not assume the role of a parent under the IDEA, and therefore may not, for example, provide or refuse consent for a student's initial evaluation or reevaluation, or provide, refuse, or revoke consent for services under the IDEA or serve as the parent on an IEP Team. It may be difficult for some parents to participate in person in IEP Team meetings if the correctional facility is not located near the parent's residence. Nevertheless, the parent participation requirements in 34 CFR §300.322 are fully applicable to public agencies that are responsible for educating students with disabilities in correctional facilities.[37] See footnote 18 for further discussion regarding use of video conferences and conference calls.

In many States, the public agency with the responsibility for the appointment of a surrogate parent is the LEA. In carrying out this responsibility, the LEA must have a method for determining whether a student needs a surrogate parent and for assigning a surrogate parent to the student (34 CFR §300.519(b)). The IDEA also permits a judge overseeing the case of a student who is a ward of the State to appoint a surrogate parent (34 CFR §300.519(c)). A surrogate parent must meet certain requirements, including that the individual not be an employee of the SEA, the LEA, or any other agency that is involved in the education or care of the student (34 CFR §300.519(d) and (e)). However, public agencies must not assume that all students with disabilities in correctional facilities need a surrogate parent. Rather, a surrogate parent acts in place of a student's parent only when: (1) the parent cannot be identified; (2) the parent cannot be located after reasonable efforts; (3) the student is a ward of the State under the laws of that State; or (4) the student is an unaccompanied or homeless youth, as defined in section 725(6) of the McKinney-Vento Homeless Assistance Act (42 U.S.C. §11434(a)(6)) (34 CFR §300.519(a)).

If parental rights transfer to students with disabilities who have reached the age of majority under State law (except for a student with a disability determined to be incompetent under State law), the public agency must provide any notices required by the IDEA, Part B regulations to both the student and the parents, and all rights accorded to parents under IDEA, Part B transfer to the student (34 CFR §§300.320(c) and 300.520(a)(3)). Therefore, it is important that public agencies are aware of the applicable law in their State governing whether parental rights transfer and provide the required notices to the student and his or her parents.

Reentry Considerations

Reentry services promote the effective reintegration of students back to communities upon release from correctional facilities. Evidence strongly supports the notion that juvenile offenders, both with and without disabilities, are significantly more likely to experience successful reentry into their home schools and communities if appropriate programs and supports are in place and discussed with the student prior to his or her release.[38] Many experts in the field recommend a comprehensive approach to reentry that includes individualized reentry plans, vocational and life skills training, behavior management systems and direct academic instruction. Reentry planning supports the successful reentry of students into their communities and includes information about State reentry options that may include the student's school prior to commitment in the correctional facility, charter schools, virtual schools, evening schools, adult education programs, community colleges, alternative schools for students with specific needs, schools with a dual focus on diploma/GED and career and technical education, and dual enrollment high/school/college programs. Informing students of their options is an important part of the reentry process. Methods to disseminate information regarding reentry options may include: (1) home visits; (2) information sharing between schools; (3) collaboration with community-based organizations; (4) school expos/reengagement fairs; (5) reengagement/transition centers; (6) print and electronic media; (7) collaboration with probation and parole practitioners from both public and private sectors; and (8) community wide campaigns.[39] The IDEA's requirements related to parental engagement, records sharing among public agencies, and transition planning, discussed above, complement these efforts.

On June 9, 2014, the U.S. Department of Education and the U.S. Department of Justice issued a letter addressing the Administration's efforts related to the education of students in juvenile facilities. The letter includes information on Title I, Part D of the ESEA, which is administered by the Department's Office of Elementary and Secondary Education and, among other matters, includes requirements that support juvenile correctional education and reentry. We are providing a copy of that letter and its enclosure with this letter to ensure that you and your staff are aware of this information and the resources available on this topic.

CONCLUSION

The Department is committed to supporting all students in our nation's schools, including correctional facilities, to achieve positive educational outcomes. Ensuring that students in correctional facilities are receiving a high quality education will have a clear, positive effect in reducing recidivism and increasing post-release success in higher education, employment, and other life endeavors. Providing FAPE to students with disabilities in correctional facilities is not only required by law; it is critically important to ensuring successful outcomes.

The Department strongly encourages SEAs, LEAs, and other public agencies, and correctional facilities serving students with disabilities to review their policies, procedures, and practices to verify that they are in compliance with IDEA requirements with a focus on improved educational outcomes for these students. SEAs and LEAs must, as part of their monitoring responsibilities, ensure that identified noncompliance is timely corrected. 34 CFR §300.600(e). We encourage SEAs and LEAs and other stakeholders to review the resources enclosed with this letter. We look forward to continuing to work with you to ensure that all students with disabilities, including students with disabilities in correctional facilities, have access to high-quality educational services.

If you have any questions or comments, please contact Office of Special Education Programs Education Program Specialists, Dr. Curtis Kinnard at 202-245-7472 or Curtis.Kinnard@ed.gov or Dr. Tony G. Williams at 202-245-7577 or TonyG.Williams@ed.gov.

Thank you for your support and your continued interest in improving results and ensuring equal access to educational services for students with disabilities.

Sincerely,

/s/	/s/
Melody Musgrove, Ed.D. Director Office of Special Education Programs	Michael K. Yudin Acting Assistant Secretary Office of Special Education and Rehabilitative Services

Enclosures

Resources

U.S. Department of Education

Individuals with Disabilities Education Act. Retrieved November 18, 2014 from http://idea.ed.gov/explore/view/p/%2Croot%2Cstatute%2C

Joint letter to Chief State School Officers and State Attorneys General with Attorney General Eric Holder regarding educational support for youth in the juvenile justice system, June 9, 2014. Retrieved July 11, 2014 from http://www2.ed.gov/policy/elsec/guid/secletter/140609.html

IDEA and FERPA Confidentiality Provisions. June 2014. Retrieved July 21, 2014 from http://www2.ed.gov/policy/gen/guid/ptac/pdf/idea-ferpa.pdf

Office of Special Education Programs Memorandum and Questions and Answers on Dispute Resolution, July 23, 2013. Retrieved July 11, 2014 from http://www2.ed.gov/policy/speced/guid/idea/memosdcltrs/ acccom binedosersdisputeresolutionqaf inalmemo-7-23-13.pdf

Questions and Answers on Individualized Education Programs (IEPs), Evaluations, and Reevaluations, September 2011. Retrieved July 11, 2014, from http://idea.ed.gov/explore/view/p/%2Croot%2Cdynamic%2CQa Corner%2C3%2C

Questions and Answers on Discipline Procedures, June 2009. Retrieved November 18, 2014 from http://idea.ed.gov/explore/view/p/%2Croot% 2Cdynamic%2CQaCorner%2C7%2C

Dear Colleague Letter on Education for Highly Mobile Children, July 19, 2013. Retrieved November 18, 2014 from http://www2.ed.gov/policy/ speced/guid/idea/memosdcltrs/12- 0392dclhighlymobile.pdf

U.S. Department of Justice

U.S. Department of Justice, Office of Justice Programs, Office of Juvenile Justice and Delinquency Prevention. http://www.ojjdp.gov

U.S. Department of Justice, Civil Rights Division, Special Litigation Section. http://www.justice.gov/crt/about/spl/juveniles.php

U.S. Department of Justice, Civil Rights Division, Educational Opportunities Section. http://www.justice.gov/crt/about/edu/.

Statement of Interest of the United States, G.F. v. Contra Costa Cnty., No. 3:13-cv-03667-MEJ (N.D. Cal. Feb. 13, 2014). http://www.justice.gov/ crt/about/spl/documents/contracosta soi 2-13- 14.pdf.

End Notes

[1] The definition of a correctional facility varies from State to State. For the purposes of this letter, "correctional institution" or "correctional facility" refers to juvenile justice facilities, detention facilities, jails, and prisons where students with disabilities are, or may be, confined. In addition, this letter uses the term "students with disabilities" to refer to children with disabilities, as that term is defined in 34 CFR §300.8.

[2] The requirements in 34 CFR §300.2(b)(1)(iv) and (2) and 34 CFR §300.154 govern the responsibilities of noneducational public agencies for the education of students with disabilities in correctional facilities.

[3] The rights of students with disabilities in correctional facilities are also protected by two other Federal laws: Section 504 of the Rehabilitation Act of 1973 (Section 504), which prohibits disability discrimination in programs or activities of entities, such as public schools and correctional agencies, that receive Federal financial assistance (29 U.S.C. §794, 34 CFR part 104); and Title II of the Americans with Disabilities Act of 1990 (Title II), which prohibits disability discrimination by public entities, including public schools and correctional agencies, regardless of whether they receive Federal financial assistance (42 U.S.C. §§12131-12134, 28 CFR part 35). For more information about these civil rights laws, see the OCR Dear Colleague Letter (dated June 9, 2014), available at http://www.ed.gov/blog/wp-content/uploads/2014/06/doj-dod-ltr.pdf

[4] Statement of Interest for the United States, G.F. v. Contra Costa County, No. 3:13-cv-03667-MEJ (N.D. Cal.) (filed Feb. 13, 2014), available at http://www.justice.gov/crt/about/spl/documents/contracosta_soi_2-13-14.pdf.

[5] Quinn, M., Rutherford, R., Leone, P., Osher, D., & Poirier, J. (2005); Center for Juvenile Justice Reform, Georgetown University, Addressing the Unmet Educational Needs of Children and Youth in the Juvenile Justice and Child Welfare Systems 2012 Edition http://cjjr.georgetown.edu/ resources2/cjjrpublications/educationpaper.html

[6] U.S. Department of Education, EDFacts Data Warehouse (EDW), OMB # 1875-0240: "IDEA, Part B Child Count and Educational Environments Collection," 2012. The definition of "correctional facilities" for this data collection is "children who received special education in correctional facilities. These data are intended to be an unduplicated count of all children receiving special education in short-term detention facilities (community-based or residential) or correctional facilities."

[7] Richard A. Mendel, No Place for Kids: The Case for Reducing Juvenile Incarceration, Annie E. Casey Foundation (2011).

[8] Mary M. Quinn, Robert B. Rutherford, Peter E. Levine, David M. Osher, and Jeffrey M. Poirier, Youth with Disabilities in Juvenile Corrections: A National Survey, Exceptional Children, Vol 71, No. 3, pp. 339-345 (2005).

[9] Robert Balfanz, Kurt Spiridakis, Ruth C. Neild, and Nettie Legters, High-Poverty Secondary School and Juvenile Justice Systems: How Neither Helps the Other and How That Could Change, 99 New Directions for Youth Development 71-89 (2003).

[10] There are some provisions of the IDEA that are not applicable to certain students with disabilities in correctional facilities. With respect to students with disabilities aged 18 through 21 in adult correctional facilities, the obligation to make FAPE available does not apply to the extent that State law does not require that special education and related services be provided to students with disabilities who, in the last educational placement prior to their incarceration in an adult correctional facility were not actually identified as being a student with a disability under the IDEA and did not have an IEP under the IDEA (34 CFR

§300.102(a)(2)(i)). However, this exception does not apply where: (1) the student with a disability, aged 18 through 21, had been identified as a student with a disability and had received services in accordance with an IEP, but left school prior to his or her incarceration, or (2) did not have an IEP in his or her last educational setting, but had been actually identified as a student with a disability (34 CFR §300.102(a)(2)(ii)).

In addition, under 34 CFR §300.324(d), for otherwise eligible students with disabilities who have been convicted as adults under State law and incarcerated in adult prisons: (1) States and LEAs are not required to include such students in State and districtwide assessments under section 612(a)(16) of the IDEA and §300.320(a)(6); (2) the requirements in §300.320(b) (relating to transition planning and transition services) do not apply with respect to the students whose eligibility under IDEA, Part B will end, because of their age, before they will be eligible to be released from prison based on consideration of their sentence and eligibility for early release; and (3) the IEP Team of a student with a disability may modify the student's IEP or placement if the State has demonstrated a bona fide security or compelling penological interest that cannot otherwise be accommodated including the requirements of §§300.320 (relating to IEPs) and 300.112 (relating to LRE).

As referenced above, under 34 CFR §300.324(d), the requirements in §300.320(b) (relating to transition planning and transition services) do not apply with respect to the students whose eligibility under IDEA, Part B will end, because of their age, before they will be eligible to be released from prison based on consideration of their sentence and eligibility for early release that apply to otherwise eligible students with disabilities who have been convicted as adults under State law and incarcerated in adult prisons. In addition, the IDEA makes no specific provision for funding educational services for individuals with disabilities incarcerated in a Federal prison. See Letter to Yudien, (August 19, 2003). https://www2.ed.gov/policy/speced/guid/idea/letters/2003-3/yudien081903fape3q2003.pdf.

[11] The definition of "State" includes the District of Columbia, the Commonwealth of Puerto Rico, and each of the outlying areas (34 CFR §300.40).

[12] Under 34 CFR §300.154(b)(1)(i), a "noneducational public agency" is described as "any public agency that is otherwise obligated under Federal or State law, or assigned responsibility under State policy, or pursuant to [§300.154(a)] to provide or pay for any services that are also considered special education or related services."

[13] The Governor, or another individual pursuant to State law, may assign to any public agency in the State the responsibility for ensuring that the requirements of IDEA are met with respect to students with disabilities who are convicted as adults under State law and incarcerated in an adult prison (34 CFR §300.149(d)). However, such an assignment does not relieve the State, or the assigned public agency, of its responsibility to meet all the requirements of IDEA, even if the public agency does not receive IDEA, Part B funds (34 CFR §300.2(b)(2)). This letter does not address the circumstances covered by 34 CFR §300.149(d).

[14] A State may also meet this requirement through other appropriate written methods, as approved by the Chief Executive Officer of a State, or his or her designee and approved by the U.S. Department of Education (34 CFR §300.154(c)(3)).

[15] Under 34 CFR §300.154(b)(1)(i), a noneducational public agency, including the State Medicaid agency and other public insurers of children with disabilities, may be assigned the responsibility to pay for special education and related services. In that case, the financial responsibility of the noneducational public agency precedes the financial responsibility of the LEA (or the State agency responsible for developing the child's IEP) (34 CFR §300.154(a)(1)). Even though these statutory and regulatory provisions specifically refer to

the State Medicaid agency or other public insurers of students with disabilities, they are equally applicable to any noneducational public agency that is otherwise obligated under State or Federal law to provide or pay for special education and related services. This requirement includes the corrections context where an agency other than an SEA or LEA is responsible for providing or paying for special education and related services.

[16] If a noneducational public agency fails to provide or pay for special education and related services, the LEA (or, if applicable, the State agency) responsible for developing the student's IEP must provide or pay for these services in a timely manner. The LEA or State agency may then claim reimbursement pursuant to the terms of the interagency agreement or other mechanism for interagency coordination (34 CFR §300.154(b)(2)).

[17] A parent and a public agency may agree to use alternative means of satisfying the IEP Team meeting participation requirements, such as through video conferences and conference calls. (34 CFR §300.328).

[18] This requirement does not apply to students in correctional facilities who have been convicted as adults under State law and incarcerated in adult prisons.

[19] In addition, as the IDEA, Part B grantee, each State must provide auditors and Department officials with access to financial and programmatic records, supporting documents, statistical records, and other records under program regulations or the grant agreement, and maintain such records and documents to facilitate an audit and to demonstrate compliance with program requirements (34 CFR §§76.730 through 76.731). See also 2 CFR 200.302(b)(3).

[20] However, there is no obligation for States to identify and evaluate those students with disabilities in adult correctional facilities for whom the State is otherwise not required to provide FAPE.

[21] For further information regarding collaborative efforts to support youth with disabilities in the juvenile justice system, see http://csgjusticecenter. org/youth/publications/addressing-the-unmet-educational-needs-of-children-andyouth-in-the-juvenile-justice-and-child-welfare-systems-2/

[22] If a student with a disability (who had an IEP that was in effect in a previous public agency in the same State) transfers to a new public agency in the same State, and enrolls in a new school within the same school year, the new public agency (in consultation with the parents) must provide FAPE to the student (including services comparable to those described in the student's IEP from the previous public agency), until the new public agency either: (1) adopts the student's IEP from the previous public agency; or (2) develops, adopts, and implements a new IEP that meets the applicable requirements in 34 CFR §§300.320 through 300.324 (34 CFR §300.323(e)). If a student with a disability (who had an IEP that was in effect in a previous public agency in another State) is moved to a correctional facility in a new State within the same school year, the new public agency (in consultation with the parents) must provide the student with FAPE (including services comparable to those described in the student's IEP from the previous public agency), until the new public agency: (1) conducts an evaluation pursuant to 34 CFR §§300.304 through 300.306 (if determined to be necessary by the new public agency); and (2) develops, adopts, and implements a new IEP, if appropriate, that meets the applicable requirements in 34 CFR §§300.320 through 300.324 (34 CFR §300.323(f)).

[23] The Family Educational Rights and Privacy Act (FERPA), 20 U.S.C. 1232g; 34 CFR part 99, generally requires that school districts and schools obtain the prior written consent of a parent or eligible student (i.e., a student 18 years of age or older or enrolled in a postsecondary institution) before disclosing personally identifiable information from

education records; however, there are a number of exceptions to this prior consent requirement. The IDEA also contains confidentiality of information provisions that require prior written consent for disclosure of personally identifiable information from education records and that generally incorporate the FERPA exceptions to the prior consent requirement. 20 U.S.C. 1417(c) and 34 CFR §300.622. The FERPA exception to the prior consent requirement that would be most relevant to a school district's or school's disclosure of education records of students who are entering a correctional facility is in 34 CFR §§99.31(a)(2) and 99.34 of FERPA regulations, which permits schools and school districts that are subject to FERPA to disclose personally identifiable information from education records without prior written consent to officials of another school or school district, including a school or school district run by a juvenile justice agency, where a student is enrolled, or seeks or intends to enroll, so long as the disclosure is for purposes related to the student's enrollment or transfer. See http://www2.ed.gov/policy/gen/guid/ptac/pdf/idea-ferpa.pdf for further clarification regarding the IDEA and FERPA confidentiality provisions and the transmission of education records to the correctional facility.

[24] See Reentry Myth Buster on Student Records, Federal Interagency Reentry Council, June 2013. http://csgjusticecenter.org/wp-content/uploads/2013/06/Student-Records.pdf.

[25] See Questions and Answers on Individualized Education Programs (IEPs), Evaluations, and Reevaluations. Retrieved July 11, 2014, from http://idea.ed.gov/explore/view/p/%2Croot%2Cdynamic%2CQaCorner%2C3%2C

[26] See Office of Special Education Programs' Dear Colleague Letter on Education for Highly Mobile Children, July 19, 2013, for a more thorough discussion of IDEA requirements applicable when students transfer. http://www2.ed.gov/policy/speced/guid/idea/memosdcltrs/12-0392dclhighlymobile.pdf

[27] See the Personnel Qualifications section discussed above.

[28] In States that have opted to make available FAPE to students with disabilities convicted as an adult under State law and incarcerated in an adult prison, the LEA may modify an IEP for such a student if the State has demonstrated a bona fide security or compelling penological interest that cannot otherwise be accommodated (34 CFR §300.324(d)(2)).

[29] Please see fn. 11 for a discussion of the responsibility to make FAPE available to students with disabilities aged 18 through 21 in adult correctional facilities.

[30] Transition services requirements are not applicable to students with disabilities in adult prisons and to students whose eligibility for IDEA services will end, because of their age, before they will be eligible to be released from prison based on consideration of their sentence and eligibility for early release (34 CFR §300.324(d)(1)(ii)).

[31] Students with disabilities in correctional facilities should already be participating as a member of the IEP Team, where appropriate (34 CFR §300.321(a)(7)). Because students with disabilities in a correctional facility are physically in the facility where the IEP Team is likely to be meeting, absent a significant medical or security concern that cannot be accommodated, the student should be participating as a member of the IEP Team, as such participation is likely to improve the student's cooperation and should assist the IEP Team in identifying the special education and related services that must be included in the IEP.

[32] Statement of Interest for the United States, G.F. v. Contra Costa County, No. 3:13-cv-03667-MEJ (N.D. Cal.) (filed Feb. 13, 2014), available at http://www.justice.gov/crt/about/spl/documents/contracosta_soi_2-13-14.pdf.

[33] Honig v. Doe, 484 U.S. 305 (1988); see also Office of Special Education and Rehabilitative Services, Questions and Answers on Discipline Procedures, June 2009, http://idea.ed.gov/explore/view/p/%2Croot%2Cdynamic%2CQaCorner%2C7%2C for a detailed discussion

of the discipline procedures applicable to children with disabilities, including the requirements related to functional behavioral assessments in 34 CFR §300.530(d)(1)(ii) and (f)(1)(i).

[34] Under 34 CFR §300.536, a change of placement because of disciplinary removals occurs if the removal from the child's current educational placement is for more than 10 consecutive school days, or if the public agency determines, on a case-by-case basis, that a pattern of removals constitutes a change of placement because the series of removals total more than 10 school days in a school year; the student's behavior is substantially similar to the behavior that resulted in the previous removals; and because of such additional factors as the length of each removal, the total amount of time the student has been removed, and the proximity of the removals to one another. The public agency may consider any unique circumstances, on a case-by-case basis, when determining whether a pattern of removals constitutes a change in placement under 34 CFR §300.536 (34 CFR §300.530(a)). The Department believes that "unique circumstances" are best determined at the local level by school personnel who know the individual child and are familiar with the facts and circumstances regarding a child's behavior. "Factors such as a child's disciplinary history, ability to understand consequences, expression of remorse, and supports provided ... prior to the violation of a school code [of student conduct] could be unique circumstances considered by school personnel when determining whether a disciplinary change in placement is appropriate for a child with a disability." 71 Fed. Reg. 46540, 46714 (Aug 14, 2006).

[35] The definition of parent is in 34 CFR §300.30.

[36] If the native language or other mode of communication of the parent is not a written language, the public agency must take steps to ensure: (1) that the notice is translated orally or by other means to the parent in his or her native language or other mode of communication; (2) that the parent understands the content of the notice; and (3) that there is written evidence that these requirements have been met. (34 CFR §300.503(c)(2)).

[37] If neither parent can attend an IEP Team meeting, the LEA or other responsible public agency must use other methods to ensure parent participation, including individual or conference telephone calls consistent with §300.328 (related to alternative means of meeting participation) (34 CFR §300.322(c)), and the public agency must maintain required documentation when the IEP Team meeting is conducted without either parent in attendance if the public agency is unable to convince the parent to attend (34 CFR §300.322(d)). Moreover, the public agency must take whatever action is necessary to ensure that the parents understand IEP Team meeting proceedings, including arranging for an interpreter for parents with deafness or whose native language is other than English (34 CFR §300.322(e)).

[38] Reentry Programs for Students with Disabilities in the Juvenile Justice System: Four State Approaches, National Association of State Directors of Special Education (NASDSE), December 2011. See also National Institute of Justice, Office of Justice Programs, for resources related to reentry. http://www.crimesolutions.gov/TopicDetails.aspx?ID=2

[39] For further information regarding strategies to reenroll youth with disabilities after exiting the correctional system, see Reentry Programs for Out of School Youth with Disabilities, Julia Wilkins, National Drop Out Center for Students with Disabilities, July 2011, and A Reentry Education Model Supporting Education and Career Advancement for Low-Skill Individuals in Corrections at http://www2.ed.gov/about/offices/list/ovae/pi/AdultEd/reentry-model.pdf. For information regarding funding opportunities for reentry programs, see http://www.ojjdp.gov/funding/FundingList.asp.

INDEX

D

E

F

G

H

I

J

K

L

M

N

U

V

W

Y